Test Practice
Grade Five
Table of Content

MW00977740

Skills Tested on Standardized Tests
for Grade 5

	CAT/5 (Level 16)	CTBS (Book B)	ITBS (Level 11)	MAT/7 (Inter 1)	SAT (9th ed) (Inter 2)	TerraNova (Level 16)	TAAS (Level B)
Vocabulary							
Identifying Synonyms	X	X	X	X	X	X	
Identifying Antonyms	X	X					
Understanding Word Meaning	X						
Identifying Word Origins	X	X					
Recognizing Words in Context	X	X	X	X	X		
Analyzing Affixes and Roots	X	X					
Understanding Multiple Meanings	X			X	X		
Reading Comprehension Skills							
Identifying Passage Details			X	X	X	X	
Determining Sequence of Events	X	X	X	X	X	X	X
Understanding Word Meaning from Context							
Understanding Cause and Effect	X	X	X	X	X	X	X
Understanding Character Traits	X	X	X	X	X	X	
Identifying Main Idea	X	X	X	X			X
Identifying Supporting Details	X	X		X	X		X
Predicting Outcomes	X	X	X	X		X	X
Distinguishing Between Fact and Opinion	X	X			X	X	X
Recognizing Genre	X		X		X		X
Analyzing Author's Purpose	X		X		X	X	
Drawing Conclusions	X			X	X	X	X
Language Mechanics and Expression							
Identifying Correct Spelling	X	X	X	X	X	X	X
Using Capitalization and Punctuation	X	X	X	X	X	X	X
Identifying Misspelled Words	X	X	X	X	X	X	X
Determining Correct Usage	X	X	X	X		X	X
Identifying Subject and Predicate	X	X					X
Combining Sentences	X	X				X	
Identifying Topic Sentences	X	X		X	X	X	
Identifying Supporting Sentences	X	X		X	X	X	
Analyzing Paragraphs			X	X	X		

www.svschoolsupply.com
© Steck-Vaughn Company
Test Practice 5, SV 3789-5

Skills Tested on Standardized Tests
for Grade 5

	CAT/5 (Level 15)	CTBS (Book B)	ITBS (Level 11)	MAT/7 (Inter 1)	SAT (9th ed) (Inter 2)	TerraNova (Level 15)	TAAS (Level B)
Mathematics Computation							
Using Computation	X	X	X	X	X	X	X
(Adding, Subtracting, Multiplying, Dividing)	X	X	X	X	X	X	X
Mathematics Concepts/Applications							
Understanding Numeration	X	X	X	X		X	X
Using Probability and Statistics	X			X	X	X	X
Working with Graphs, Charts, and Tables	X	X	X	X			X
Understanding Measurement and Geometry	X	X	X	X	X	X	X
Working with Number Sentences	X	X	X	X		X	
Using Estimation	X		X		X	X	
Understanding Number Theory	X		X		X	X	
Working with Algebra					X	X	
Understanding Mathematics Relationships	X		X	X	X	X	X
Mathematics Problem-Solving							
Using Problem-Solving Strategies	X			X	X	X	X
Solving Word Problems	X	X	X	X		X	X
Study Skills							
Understanding Book Parts	X	X	X	X	X		
Using the Dictionary	X	X	X	X	X		
Using Reference Materials	X		X	X	X		
Organizing Information	X	X		X	X		
Analyzing Visual Information	X	X	X				
Using the Library		X	X				

Standardized achievement testing is a fact of life in public and private schools. As the United States continues moving toward applying national standards for achievement at each grade level, standardized testing will take on even greater importance to the public. Expectations for education are changing throughout the country as performance standards for students in all grades are being raised. The high-tech world of the twenty-first century will require that students acquire more sophisticated reading, writing, and math skills. Evaluation of how well the schools are helping our students to meet the new national standards is the primary focus of many standardized achievement test programs.

With so much emphasis on the goal of achieving high test scores, it's not surprising that some teachers and administrators feel apprehensive when test schedules are announced. In turn, this sense of apprehension is often transmitted to their students. How can we make standardized test-taking a positive educational experience for students? Teachers and parents can familiarize themselves with the format of, the skills covered by, and the test language used in the standardized tests used in their schools. Teachers and administrators are often asked, "What's on the test?" Though specific answers to that question are not available, teachers and parents should be knowledgeable about what skills students are expected to know as they progress through school. Teachers and parents can give students the tools to assist them in improving test-taking skills. Students can be taught how to read and listen to directions, how to use an answer sheet, how to budget their time during a timed test, and even how to control test stress.

Standardized Achievement Tests

Though there are many standardized tests available, the following tests are administered in grades 2–6, cover the test areas of vocabulary, reading comprehension, spelling, language, mathematics, and study skills, and were selected as the basis of this test practice series. The CAT/5 is the *California Achievement Tests, Fifth Edition*. The CTBS is the *Comprehensive Tests of Basic Skills*. The ITBS is the *Iowa Tests of Basic Skills*. The MAT/7 is the *Metropolitan Achievement Tests, Seventh Edition*. The SAT is the *Stanford Achievement Test, Ninth Edition*. The TAAS is the *Texas Assessment of Academic Skills*. The *TerraNova* is the new replacement for the CTBS and is the most recent achievement test to reach the school market.

Interpreting and Reporting Test Results

The standardized tests that elementary students frequently take, as noted on the Skills/Achievement Tests Grid on pages 2–3, are norm-referenced tests. These tests are administered in uniform testing conditions, and they compare the performance of the student to a representative sample of students from the nation's public schools. The test results are generally provided in percentile form. For example, suppose a student scores in the 68th percentile. This indicates that this student performs better than 67% of all the students in the national sample—and not as well as 31% of the students in the sample. In many school districts, parents receive standardized test results for their children either at parent conferences or through written communication. School districts often report test results by individual schools for local publication in newspapers. States sometimes compare the scores of individual school districts. Standardized tests provide one measure of students' academic progress. Standardized test results are most effective when used in conjunction with classroom assessments, which are more diagnostic in nature.

ORGANIZATION

This book contains seven units, and each unit focuses on a specific test-taking skill area: Vocabulary, Reading Comprehension, Language Mechanics and Expression, Mathematics Computation, Mathematics Concepts/Applications, Mathematics Problem-Solving, and Study Skills. These seven skill areas were selected by comparing the components of the commonly used standardized tests listed in the Skills/Achievement Tests Grid on pages 2 and 3. You can use this Skills/Achievement

Test Practice
Grade Five
Introduction

Tests Grid to review which skills students are generally expected to know by the end of the fifth grade. This will enable you to plan practice lessons emphasizing those skills. Check the Skills/Achievement Tests Grid for the standardized tests that your school will be using.

The main test areas included in this series are described below. For more definitions of testing terms, refer to the list of definitions on page 7.

- **Vocabulary**
  This test measures a student's knowledge of synonyms and antonyms. The emphasis now is on measuring a student's ability to make use of a reading selection containing multiple meanings of words and word affixes.
- **Reading Comprehension**
  This test measures a student's basic understanding of the meaning of an informational passage, a narrative selection, or a poem. Going beyond the literal comprehension level, the emphasis is on measuring a student's ability to interpret, analyze, and evaluate text using such skills as making inferences, drawing conclusions, and predicting outcomes.
- **Language Mechanics and Expression**
  These tests emphasize the writing process. The Language Mechanics test focuses on the ability to handle the editing process, including identifying correct spelling, using capitalization and punctuation conventions, demonstrating knowledge of subject and predicate, and demonstrating correct usage. The Language Expression test measures sentence and paragraph development, use of topic sentences and supporting details, ability to combine sentences, and understanding of writing conventions.
- **Mathematics Computation**
  This test measures the fundamental operations of basic math instruction by testing a student's ability to demonstrate proficiency in the computation procedures of addition, subtraction, multiplication, and division.

- **Mathematics Concepts/Applications**
  This test measures the ability to demonstrate an understanding of numbers and number relationships, including the ability to use probability and statistics and to apply concepts to visual representations of problems.
- **Mathematics Problem-Solving**
  This test evaluates a student's ability to apply problem-solving strategies to identify information, use patterns and relationships, apply estimation strategies, and solve computation problems.
- **Study Skills**
  This test measures a student's demonstrated proficiency in using various reference materials and information processing skills.

Parallel Tests
This book includes two parallel forms of each test because some students need more practice than do others. You might decide to use one form as a pretest and the parallel form as a posttest. Or, you might photocopy Form A of a test and use it for both a pretest and a posttest, while using Form B in daily practice sessions between administering pre- and posttests. Or, you might choose to use one form as homework assignments, sending one test home at a time.

Record Forms
- The Individual Record Form on page 8 can help you summarize each student's strengths and weaknesses in the specific skills of a test and help you decide what skills a student should practice further.
- Completing the Class Record Form on page 9 will give you an overview of skill areas for planning appropriate instructional activities for small groups or an entire class.
- The Answer Sheet on pages 123–124 is a separate bubble-in form that follows the last test. Remove this form and photocopy it for each student to use with each test. The Answer Key, for the teacher's use only, begins on page 125.

Test Practice
Grade Five
Introduction

USE

The *Test Practice* series is designed for independent use by students who have had prior instruction in the specific skills covered in the tests. These tests are intended as practice to get students feeling more comfortable with the test-taking environment and procedures. Copies of the tests can be given to individuals, to pairs of students, to small groups, or to an entire class. They can also be used as homework or as a center activity.

To begin, decide the implementation that fits your students' needs and your classroom structure. The following plan suggests one format for implementation:

1. <u>Review</u> the tips below.
2. <u>Send</u> the Letter to Parents on page 10 home with students so family members can help.
3. <u>Review</u> the Skills/Achievement Tests Grid on pages 2–3 to know the skills included. Then check the Table of Contents to locate which test you'd like to administer. Photocopy those pages and the Answer Sheet on pages 123–124.
4. <u>Explain</u> the purpose of the practice test to your students. Review with students the procedures for how you want them to conduct themselves during the test; see the tips below.
5. <u>Do</u> a sample item together and discuss it.
6. <u>Use</u> a timer to time the students during the test; monitor them also. Assure them that these pages are for practice purposes only, and they are to do their best.
7. <u>Use</u> the Answer Key on pages 125–128 to check students' answers. Then record the scores on the record forms on pages 8–9.

Getting Started: Tips for Teachers

Here are some helpful ideas for teachers to do before administering a standardized test. Discuss test-taking strategies in general with students with emphasis on these points:

- The test is timed; practice using the time efficiently. Practice using a timer to begin and end activities of 10–20 minutes.

- Practice ways to avoid making errors, such as looking closely at item numbers and corresponding answer sheet numbers or completely erasing a wrong answer.
- Be sure that students understand the directions for each test before they begin to work independently. Complete sample items together and discuss the thought process for selecting each answer. Discuss how to apply logical reasoning to choose the best answer choice.
- Discuss when and how to guess.
- Decide how many days per week you will practice test-taking skills and plan accordingly.
- Set aside a sufficient block of time for each test you plan to administer. Use the time limits printed at the end of each test as your guide.
- Make your room environment as close to a real test situation as possible.
- Ask students to sit in separate desks and to spread out.
- Remind them not to talk during the test.
- Put a "Testing—Do Not Disturb" sign on the door.

Tips for Students

Here are some tips to discuss and practice with your students before they take a standardized test.
- Stay calm. Focus on the task.
- Look over the entire test section before beginning.
- Read all the answer choices before choosing one.
- Have some scratch paper on hand for math problems.
- Complete all the test questions, but don't spend too much time on any one item.
- Do not ask questions during the test.
- Check to be sure the test question numbers match the answer sheet numbers.
- Take all the time allowed; reread the questions and your answers if you finish early.

Here are some terms to know concerning standardized achievement testing.

achievement test A test that measures student knowledge resulting from specific instruction.

age equivalent The score derived from age norms on a standardized test established by determining the average score made by students of each age.

age norms The typical or average performance on standardized tests for students in different age groups.

criterion-referenced test The measurement of proficiency in specific curriculum areas by evaluating a student's degree of success in completing prescribed tasks; it tells what a student is able to do.

deviation The difference between one set of values/scores and the mean.

diagnostic test A test used to discover the nature and, if possible, the causes of inability to perform average scholastic tasks.

frequency distribution A table for classifying test scores according to the number of times they occur in a group evaluation.

grade equivalent The score derived from grade norms on a standardized test.

grade norm The mean raw score obtained by students in a particular grade.

intelligence test A series of tests that measures general mental ability or scholastic aptitude.

mean The point on a scale above and below which the deviations are equal.

median The point on a scale below which half of the scores in a frequency distribution fall.

norm-referenced test A test based on standards determined by testing a large number of students of different age or grade placement; it tells how a student compares with others.

percentile rank The position assigned to a score when the scores are divided into one hundred equal divisions in descending order.

portfolio assessment This method of tracking a student's progress involves selecting chronological samples of a student's work that can be compared to show the progress over time and storing the samples in a folder.

reliability The consistency in test results; the degree to which a test's results actually measure what a student can do on a given test.

rubric A scoring guide based on a scale for rating a group of students' papers.

standardized test A test for which norms on a reference group are provided; a test with specific procedures such that comparable measurements may be made by testers in different geographic areas.

stanine One of nine standard divisions of test scores with the fifth stanine representing the average or mean score and a standard deviation of two.

validity The degree to which a test measures what it is designed to measure, or that it can predict performance on other measures.

Name _____ Date _____ Form _____

Individual Record Form

	Number Correct	Retest?
Vocabulary		
Synonyms, Antonyms, Homonyms, Word Meaning		
Words in Context, Multiple Meanings		
Affixes, Word Origins		
Reading Comprehension		
Main Idea, Supporting Details		
Author's Purpose, Genre, Predicting		
Cause & Effect, Conclusions, Sequence		
Fact & Opinion, Character		
Language Mechanics and Expression		
Spelling, Capitalization, Punctuation		
Usage, Subject, Predicate		
Sentence Combining, Paragraph Analysis		
Topic Sentences, Supporting Statements		
Mathematics Computation		
Basic Computation		
Mathematics Concepts/Applications		
Numeration, Probability & Statistics		
Graphs, Charts, Tables		
Mathematics Problem-Solving		
Fractions, Money, Measurement, Geometry		
Number Sentences, Estimation		
Algebra, Number Sentences		
Number Theory, Mathematics Relationships		
Study Skills		
Dictionary, Reference Materials		
Library, Book Parts		
Visual Information, Organizing Information		

Class Record Form

Form _____

Students	Vocabulary	Reading Comprehension	Language Mechanics and Expression	Mathematics Computation	Mathematics Concepts/Applications	Mathematics Problem-Solving	Study Skills

www.svschoolsupply.com
© Steck-Vaughn Company

Test Practice 5, SV 3789-5

Dear Parent,

At some time during this school year, our class will be taking standardized tests. Because we want children to be familiar with the format and language of the tests they will likely be taking, from time to time we will practice with sample tests. Test-taking can be a stressful experience for many children. By giving them the tools to help them feel comfortable, we can reduce their stress level.

Please consider the following suggestions for helping your child perform as well as he or she is able on the test:
• See that your child gets a good night's sleep, especially on the night before a test.
• Make sure he or she eats a healthy breakfast.
• Review any content areas that your child might feel uncertain about.
• Practice with your child the use of a timer to start and end an activity.
• Remind your child about general test-taking strategies, such as:
    – stay calm and focus on the task
    – listen to or read all the directions
    – look over the entire test or section before beginning
    – read all the answer choices before choosing one
    – don't spend too much time on any one item
    – take all the time allowed; look back over your answers.

If your child expresses anxiety about taking the tests, talk about what might be causing these feelings. Then talk about ways to overcome these feelings. Above all, assure your child that the practice tests provide an opportunity for him or her to improve skills that will help when the actual tests are given. Having your support plus the knowledge of good test-taking skills will go a long way toward improving your child's standardized test scores.

Thank you for your help!

Cordially,

Test 1: Vocabulary, Part One (Form A)

Directions For questions 1–8 darken the circle for the word or group of words that means the *same* or *almost the same* as the underlined word.

Sample A

A summary of events
- Ⓐ report
- Ⓑ brief account
- Ⓒ essay
- Ⓓ composition

Time: 18 minutes

1. A sturdy rope
   - Ⓐ strong
   - Ⓑ long
   - Ⓒ thin
   - Ⓓ twisted

2. Ancient equipment
   - Ⓐ used
   - Ⓑ discarded
   - Ⓒ obsolete
   - Ⓓ useful

3. Conceal information
   - Ⓐ store
   - Ⓑ hide
   - Ⓒ find
   - Ⓓ reveal

4. Check with the authorities
   - Ⓐ officials
   - Ⓑ people
   - Ⓒ salespeople
   - Ⓓ students

5. Resolved to do better
   - Ⓐ determined
   - Ⓑ failed
   - Ⓒ happy
   - Ⓓ cared

6. Distinctive features
   - Ⓐ pretty
   - Ⓑ ordinary
   - Ⓒ particular
   - Ⓓ common

7. Move rapidly
   - Ⓐ lazily
   - Ⓑ swiftly
   - Ⓒ loudly
   - Ⓓ happily

8. Appeal for help
   - Ⓐ offer
   - Ⓑ sing
   - Ⓒ reason
   - Ⓓ ask

GO ON ⇨

Test 1: Vocabulary, Part One
(Form A), page 2

Directions For questions 9–16 darken the circle for the word that means the *opposite* of the underlined word.

Sample B

To <u>damage</u> machinery
- Ⓐ break
- Ⓑ build
- Ⓒ replace
- Ⓓ repair

9. A <u>fair</u> decision
- Ⓐ recent
- Ⓑ unjust
- Ⓒ correct
- Ⓓ unclear

10. A bank <u>deposit</u>
- Ⓐ withdrawal
- Ⓑ loan
- Ⓒ mortgage
- Ⓓ statement

11. A <u>melancholy</u> song
- Ⓐ tuneful
- Ⓑ jazz
- Ⓒ happy
- Ⓓ romantic

12. A <u>comical</u> story
- Ⓐ humorous
- Ⓑ serious
- Ⓒ long
- Ⓓ mysterious

13. A <u>smooth</u> road
- Ⓐ paved
- Ⓑ narrow
- Ⓒ curvy
- Ⓓ rough

14. A <u>murky</u> sky
- Ⓐ clear
- Ⓑ dark
- Ⓒ dismal
- Ⓓ cloudy

15. An <u>elegant</u> party
- Ⓐ surprise
- Ⓑ crude
- Ⓒ nice
- Ⓓ tasteful

16. A <u>chattering</u> group
- Ⓐ loud
- Ⓑ talkative
- Ⓒ noisy
- Ⓓ reserved

GO ON ⇨

Test 1: Vocabulary, Part One
(Form A), page 3

Sample C

Which word probably comes from the Italian word *banc,* meaning *a table or bench used by money exchangers*?

- Ⓐ bench
- Ⓑ bank
- Ⓒ blank
- Ⓓ bang

17. Which word probably comes from the Greek word *calamitis,* meaning *a failed wheat crop*?
- Ⓐ callous
- Ⓑ calamity
- Ⓒ cauldron
- Ⓓ caulking

18. Which word probably comes from the Latin word *praevaricor,* meaning *a farmer who makes crooked furrows and someone who gives crooked answers*?
- Ⓐ prevaricate
- Ⓑ prevail
- Ⓒ prevalent
- Ⓓ prevent

19. Which word probably comes from the French word *stationnaire,* meaning *something in a fixed place*?
- Ⓐ standard
- Ⓑ stalled
- Ⓒ station
- Ⓓ stature

20. Which word probably comes from the Norse word *berserker,* meaning *warriors who destroy anything in their way*?
- Ⓐ benefit
- Ⓑ bandit
- Ⓒ beseech
- Ⓓ berserk

21. Which word probably comes from the French word *sanitaire,* meaning *relating to health*?
- Ⓐ sanity
- Ⓑ sanitary
- Ⓒ sandiness
- Ⓓ sandman

22. Which word probably comes from two Greek words *helix,* meaning *spiral,* and *pteron,* meaning *wings*?
- Ⓐ heliotrope
- Ⓑ helmet
- Ⓒ helpful
- Ⓓ helicopter

GO ON ⇨

Test 1: Vocabulary, Part One
(Form A), page 4

Directions For questions 23–28 darken the circle for the word that best fits both sentences.

Sample D

We are _____ the number of books on each shelf.

Shari is _____ on me to help with the dinner preparations.

- Ⓐ stacking
- Ⓑ working
- Ⓒ labeling
- Ⓓ counting

---

23. Be sure to _____ the surprise gift.
Cow _____ is used for many products.
- Ⓐ buy
- Ⓑ skin
- Ⓒ hide
- Ⓓ open

24. Mavis ordered _____ meat for dinner.
Roy does not want you to _____ against that wall.
- Ⓐ broiled
- Ⓑ lean
- Ⓒ stand
- Ⓓ rare

25. Did you ever watch a potter _____ clay?
The scientists grew a new _____ in the laboratory.
- Ⓐ mold
- Ⓑ mole
- Ⓒ shape
- Ⓓ experiment

26. We'll get more shelving at the _____ yard.
Watch that elephant _____ slowly down the road.
- Ⓐ ship
- Ⓑ school
- Ⓒ lumber
- Ⓓ boat

27. That is a very _____ piece of yarn.
I _____ for the time when I can visit my grandparents.
- Ⓐ nice
- Ⓑ wait
- Ⓒ hope
- Ⓓ long

28. What did you _____ by that statement?
That is a _____ looking animal.
- Ⓐ mean
- Ⓑ ask
- Ⓒ sorry
- Ⓓ want

STOP

STOP

Test 1: Vocabulary, Part Two (Form A)

Directions For questions 1–6 darken the circle for the word that best completes each sentence in the paragraph.

Sample A

A long time ago when our nation was still __**S1**__ west, the settlers had to rely on one another in order to __**S2**__. This was especially true when new families arrived in the area.

S1. Ⓐ marching
Ⓑ walking
Ⓒ moving
Ⓓ riding

S2. Ⓐ survive
Ⓑ plant
Ⓒ worry
Ⓓ fight

Time: 8 minutes

To remember the face and __**1**__ of someone you just met, take a __**2**__ in your mind. Say the name __**3**__. Think about something you already know about that person.

1. Ⓐ radio
Ⓑ name
Ⓒ address
Ⓓ books

2. Ⓐ picture
Ⓑ question
Ⓒ walk
Ⓓ look

3. Ⓐ together
Ⓑ later
Ⓒ tomorrow
Ⓓ aloud

In 1998 Gladys Knight celebrated her fiftieth __**4**__ in show business. During all those years, she has __**5**__ three Grammy awards, toured the world, and had many successful single records and albums. People in the entertainment industry call her a __**6**__ legend.

4. Ⓐ birthday
Ⓑ record
Ⓒ album
Ⓓ anniversary

5. Ⓐ won
Ⓑ taken
Ⓒ made
Ⓓ worn

6. Ⓐ happy
Ⓑ living
Ⓒ walking
Ⓓ smiling

GO ON ⇨

Test 1: Vocabulary, Part Two (Form A), page 2

Directions For questions 7–16 darken the circle for the word or words that give the best meaning for the underlined prefix or suffix.

Sample B

rest<u>less</u>   fault<u>less</u>

Ⓐ not
Ⓑ without
Ⓒ between
Ⓓ twice

7. <u>non</u>sense   <u>non</u>profit
   Ⓐ more
   Ⓑ before
   Ⓒ not
   Ⓓ never

8. sens<u>ible</u>   poss<u>ible</u>
   Ⓐ can be
   Ⓑ without
   Ⓒ in what way
   Ⓓ which was

9. length<u>en</u>   weak<u>en</u>
   Ⓐ in what way
   Ⓑ can be
   Ⓒ to make
   Ⓓ without

10. techn<u>ology</u>   bi<u>ology</u>
    Ⓐ one who
    Ⓑ study of
    Ⓒ place where
    Ⓓ time when

11. <u>multi</u>tude   <u>multi</u>million
    Ⓐ able to
    Ⓑ half
    Ⓒ like
    Ⓓ many

12. <u>mis</u>named   <u>mis</u>taken
    Ⓐ wrongly
    Ⓑ not
    Ⓒ when
    Ⓓ who

13. act<u>or</u>   spectat<u>or</u>
    Ⓐ like
    Ⓑ one who
    Ⓒ towards
    Ⓓ can

14. <u>re</u>appear   <u>re</u>locate
    Ⓐ do again
    Ⓑ able to
    Ⓒ go towards
    Ⓓ without

15. <u>inter</u>act   <u>inter</u>view
    Ⓐ guess
    Ⓑ able
    Ⓒ between
    Ⓓ never

16. <u>trans</u>port   <u>trans</u>atlantic
    Ⓐ before
    Ⓑ after
    Ⓒ among
    Ⓓ across

STOP

STOP

Test 1: Vocabulary, Part One (Form B)

Directions For questions 1–8 darken the circle for the word or group of words that means the *same* or *almost the same* as the underlined word.

Sample A

<u>obscure</u> village

- Ⓐ local
- Ⓑ remote
- Ⓒ apparent
- Ⓓ peaceful

Time: 18 minutes

1. To <u>initiate</u> a program
   - Ⓐ begin
   - Ⓑ see
   - Ⓒ review
   - Ⓓ cancel

2. A <u>radiant</u> personality
   - Ⓐ active
   - Ⓑ annoying
   - Ⓒ glowing
   - Ⓓ grumpy

3. To hold a <u>grudge</u>
   - Ⓐ ill will
   - Ⓑ meeting
   - Ⓒ parade
   - Ⓓ contest

4. To <u>pursue</u> a goal
   - Ⓐ reach
   - Ⓑ test
   - Ⓒ follow
   - Ⓓ test

5. An <u>obstructed</u> view
   - Ⓐ pleasant
   - Ⓑ blocked
   - Ⓒ open
   - Ⓓ scenic

6. To <u>eliminate</u> the causes
   - Ⓐ find
   - Ⓑ understand
   - Ⓒ erase
   - Ⓓ change

7. To <u>chastise</u> the criminal
   - Ⓐ arrest
   - Ⓑ punish
   - Ⓒ free
   - Ⓓ applaud

8. A <u>solemn</u> promise
   - Ⓐ serious
   - Ⓑ honest
   - Ⓒ trivial
   - Ⓓ daring

GO ON ⇨

Test 1: Vocabulary, Part One (Form B), page 2

Directions For questions 9–16 darken the circle for the word that means the *opposite* of the underlined word.

Sample B

slovenly notebook

- Ⓐ neat
- Ⓑ sloppy
- Ⓒ careless
- Ⓓ unusual

9. Running is prohibited.
   - Ⓐ allowed
   - Ⓑ happening
   - Ⓒ stopped
   - Ⓓ banned

10. Problems about work
    - Ⓐ questions
    - Ⓑ stories
    - Ⓒ solutions
    - Ⓓ examinations

11. Commence the concert
    - Ⓐ finish
    - Ⓑ start
    - Ⓒ begin
    - Ⓓ delay

12. Acquire a fortune
    - Ⓐ gain
    - Ⓑ lose
    - Ⓒ achieve
    - Ⓓ earn

13. Abundance of food
    - Ⓐ amount
    - Ⓑ quantity
    - Ⓒ serving
    - Ⓓ scarcity

14. Immense territory
    - Ⓐ vast
    - Ⓑ enormous
    - Ⓒ tiny
    - Ⓓ huge

15. Preceding program
    - Ⓐ following
    - Ⓑ previous
    - Ⓒ earlier
    - Ⓓ latest

16. Vacant store
    - Ⓐ empty
    - Ⓑ full
    - Ⓒ busy
    - Ⓓ expensive

GO ON ⇨

Directions For questions 17–22 darken the circle for the word that comes from another language.

Sample C

Which word probably comes from the Spanish word *tronada*, meaning a *thunderstorm*?

Ⓐ torment
Ⓑ torch
Ⓒ torpedo
Ⓓ tornado

17. Which word probably comes from the Latin word *fortuna*, meaning *chance*?

Ⓐ fortify
Ⓑ forty
Ⓒ fortune
Ⓓ forum

18. Which word probably comes from the French word *contraster*, meaning *to oppose*?

Ⓐ constant
Ⓑ contain
Ⓒ conform
Ⓓ contrast

19. Which word probably comes from the Middle English word *bartren*, meaning *to trade by exchanging goods*?

Ⓐ barber
Ⓑ barter
Ⓒ barrow
Ⓓ barrier

20. Which word probably comes from the Italian word *turbante*, meaning *a headdress*?

Ⓐ turmoil
Ⓑ turbine
Ⓒ turbot
Ⓓ turban

21. Which word probably comes from the Latin word *eventus*, meaning *to happen*?

Ⓐ evict
Ⓑ event
Ⓒ ventilate
Ⓓ venom

22. Which word probably comes from the Latin word *tradere*, meaning *to hand over*?

Ⓐ handle
Ⓑ trailer
Ⓒ radiant
Ⓓ traitor

GO ON ⇨

Test 1: Vocabulary, Part One
(Form B), page 4

Directions For questions 23–28 darken the circle for the word that best fits both sentences.

Sample D

A huge _____ of books fell.

The soft _____ of a rug feels good.

Ⓐ stack

Ⓑ finish

Ⓒ design

Ⓓ pile

---

23. Eva's new sweater has _____ stripes across the back.

The pirates decided to _____ their captives on a small island.

Ⓐ leave

Ⓑ maroon

Ⓒ gray

Ⓓ narrow

24. The runner's energy began to _____ .

We each wanted to carry a _____ in the parade.

Ⓐ flag

Ⓑ ebb

Ⓒ sign

Ⓓ waver

25. The view from the high _____ was awesome.

Randy tried to _____ his way out of trouble.

Ⓐ rooftop

Ⓑ talk

Ⓒ bluff

Ⓓ hilltop

26. The book is _____ in hand-tooled leather.

The train is _____ for Boston.

Ⓐ decorated

Ⓑ bound

Ⓒ heading

Ⓓ destined

27. We have to _____ the paper in equal parts.

The sheep huddled together in the _____.

Ⓐ fold

Ⓑ divide

Ⓒ field

Ⓓ cut

28. Perry brought _____ doughnuts to the picnic.

Polite people don't make _____ remarks.

Ⓐ delicious

Ⓑ rude

Ⓒ fresh

Ⓓ stale

STOP

STOP

Test 1: Vocabulary, Part Two (Form B)

Directions For questions 1–6, darken the circle for the word that best completes each sentence in the paragraph.

Sample A

In the 1600s people in England started to travel by public coach. The first trips were very ___**S1**___. They had to make frequent stops to give the ___**S2**___ a rest.

S1. Ⓐ long
   Ⓑ frequent
   Ⓒ funny
   Ⓓ scenic

S2. Ⓐ motors
   Ⓑ autos
   Ⓒ horses
   Ⓓ roads

Time: 8 minutes

Boat-building is an ___**1**___ craft. The first materials that people used probably came from ___**2**___. People learned to build many ___**3**___ kinds of boats to sail on the water.

1. Ⓐ easy
   Ⓑ ancient
   Ⓒ terrible
   Ⓓ impossible

2. Ⓐ trees
   Ⓑ flowers
   Ⓒ rubber
   Ⓓ fabric

3. Ⓐ pretty
   Ⓑ tall
   Ⓒ different
   Ⓓ normal

Long ago ships had very limited ways of communicating with each other. They had to use ___**4**___ that could only be seen or heard by ships nearby. The visual signals they used by day were ___**5**___. At night, they used ___**6**___ and blinkers.

4. Ⓐ sails
   Ⓑ signals
   Ⓒ engines
   Ⓓ questions

5. Ⓐ hands
   Ⓑ telegraphs
   Ⓒ smoke
   Ⓓ flags

6. Ⓐ radios
   Ⓑ lanterns
   Ⓒ telephones
   Ⓓ horns

GO ON ⇨

Test 1: Vocabulary, Part Two
(Form B), page 2

Directions For questions 7–16 darken the circle for the word or words that give the best meaning for the underlined prefix or suffix.

Sample B

inject   insert

Ⓐ about
Ⓑ for
Ⓒ into
Ⓓ against

7. misbehave   miscalculate
   Ⓐ like
   Ⓑ against
   Ⓒ to
   Ⓓ wrong

8. convene   concur
   Ⓐ together
   Ⓑ one who
   Ⓒ on
   Ⓓ from

9. lovable   comfortable
   Ⓐ to make
   Ⓑ without
   Ⓒ can be
   Ⓓ more than

10. rapidly   speedily
    Ⓐ towards
    Ⓑ from
    Ⓒ how
    Ⓓ like

11. octagon   October
    Ⓐ eight
    Ⓑ half
    Ⓒ two
    Ⓓ five

12. monotone   monorail
    Ⓐ same
    Ⓑ one
    Ⓒ ten
    Ⓓ four

13. thoughtless   restless
    Ⓐ again
    Ⓑ between
    Ⓒ without
    Ⓓ like

14. gigantic   heroic
    Ⓐ like
    Ⓑ full of
    Ⓒ twice
    Ⓓ lack of

15. delightful   hurtful
    Ⓐ filled with
    Ⓑ not
    Ⓒ again
    Ⓓ over

16. repack   retell
    Ⓐ about
    Ⓑ again
    Ⓒ towards
    Ⓓ like

STOP

STOP

Test 2: Reading Comprehension (Form A)

Directions For questions 1–45 read each selection. Then darken the circle for the correct answer to each question.

Sample

Some scientists are concerned about global warming. They are warning us that we must reduce the amount of carbon dioxide being released into the air. One way to do this is to stop burning fossil fuels. Instead, we should learn to use solar power and wind power. Scientists are convinced that solar power and wind power are the fuels that will be used in the twenty-first century.

1. What is concerning some scientists?
   - Ⓐ fossil fuels
   - Ⓑ wind power
   - Ⓒ global warming
   - Ⓓ the twenty-first century

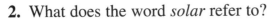

2. What does the word *solar* refer to?
   - Ⓐ fuel
   - Ⓑ Sun
   - Ⓒ fossils
   - Ⓓ global

Time: 45 minutes

Did you ever think about the ways that dogs and wolves are alike? How might they be related? One theory is that cave dwellers admired wolves for their strength, their speed, and the way they hunted. The cave dwellers decided to train wolves to help them hunt.

Through many, many centuries of breeding, taming, and training, wolves have developed into the domesticated dogs of today. Dogs still have many characteristics that they inherited from their ancestors, the wolves. For example, dogs bury bones. Wolves bury food and bones when food is scarce. Wolves are hunters. Some breeds of dogs are trained to be hunters because they have unusual senses of sight, smell, and hearing. Wolves, too, rely on these senses when they hunt. Wolves protect their packs and their territories. Some breeds of dogs, such as sheepdogs, can herd and protect flocks of sheep. Both wolves and dogs bark, although wolves don't bark as often as dogs. Wolves howl when they need to communicate with each other.

All dogs—no matter which breed— began as wolves. It's hard to imagine that even the tiniest poodle has a wolf in its family tree.

1. What does the word *domesticated* mean in this selection?
   - Ⓐ harmless
   - Ⓑ mild
   - Ⓒ frisky
   - Ⓓ trained

GO ON ⇨

Test 2: Reading Comprehension
(Form A), page 2

2. Which would be a good title for this selection?
   - Ⓐ All About Dogs
   - Ⓑ From Wolves to Dogs
   - Ⓒ Breeding Hunting Dogs
   - Ⓓ Why Wolves Howl

3. Which statement is *not* true?
   - Ⓐ Wolves don't know how to protect their packs.
   - Ⓑ Dogs like to bury bones.
   - Ⓒ Cave people trained wolves to help them hunt.
   - Ⓓ All dogs are descended from wolves.

4. What can you conclude about the author of this selection?
   - Ⓐ The author likes wolves.
   - Ⓑ The author knows a lot about dogs and wolves.
   - Ⓒ The author is a good storyteller.
   - Ⓓ The author visited many caves.

5. About how long did it take to train wolves to live with humans?
   - Ⓐ one hundred years
   - Ⓑ one generation
   - Ⓒ thousands of years
   - Ⓓ fifty years

6. Why did cave dwellers want to train wolves?
   - Ⓐ They wanted the wolves to bury food.
   - Ⓑ They wanted the wolves to protect their caves.
   - Ⓒ They wanted the wolves to stop howling.
   - Ⓓ They wanted the wolves to help them hunt.

GO ON ⇨

Test 2: Reading Comprehension (Form A), page 3

For over seventy years, Macy's, a large department store in New York City, has held a parade to kick off the start of the holiday season. People from all over the world come to see the giant balloons of their favorite TV and cartoon figures as the balloons move down the parade route. Some of the sculptures have included Sesame Street characters, Peter Rabbit, Bullwinkle, and Spiderman. Some of these balloon sculptures are as tall as a six-story building. Each figure has heavy ropes attached to it and is anchored with sandbags. The figures are led by a team of at least four people holding on to the ropes.

The night before the parade, many New Yorkers gather in Central Park to watch the balloons being inflated with helium. It takes a very long time to fill all the balloons, and the workers usually work past midnight.

On the day of the parade, crowds of people line the route very early. The parade ends at the entrance to Macy's when Santa Claus arrives on his sleigh. Most people agree that this is a very special way to begin the season.

7. What is the purpose of the sandbags?
   Ⓐ to inflate the balloons
   Ⓑ to keep the balloons from floating away
   Ⓒ to connect to the ropes
   Ⓓ to keep the balloons in Central Park

8. What does the expression *kick off* mean?
   Ⓐ start
   Ⓑ finish
   Ⓒ injure
   Ⓓ turn

9. Which holiday season is being kicked off?
   Ⓐ Valentine's Day
   Ⓑ Veterans' Day
   Ⓒ Christmas
   Ⓓ the Fourth of July

10. You can tell that New Yorkers think this is a special event because _____.
    Ⓐ There are many balloon sculptures.
    Ⓑ They like to watch the balloons being prepared the night before the parade.
    Ⓒ The balloons are six stories high.
    Ⓓ They like to see the arrival of Santa Claus.

11. A good title for this selection could be _____.
    Ⓐ I Love a Parade
    Ⓑ The Night Before Thanksgiving
    Ⓒ Getting Christmas Off to a Good Start
    Ⓓ Helium-Filled Balloons

GO ON ⇨

Test 2: Reading Comprehension
(Form A), page 4

A huge sunken tube tunnel is being built as part of a bridge-tunnel between Sweden and Denmark. It will be Sweden's first direct road and rail link to the rest of Europe.

When construction workers came to the thirteenth of twenty parts they had to install, they numbered it 12A. Changing the number didn't do any good. Part 12A sank accidentally in early August. The accident caused a two-month delay in the project.

Project officials still expect the bridge-tunnel to open in 2000. At that time the Danish capital of Copenhagen will be connected to the Swedish port city of Malmö. Instead of taking a ferry from Sweden to Denmark, people will be able to drive from one country to another!

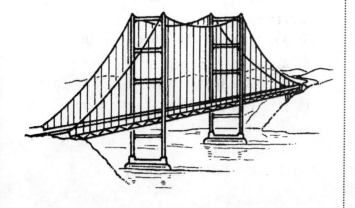

12. Why did the workers change the number on the thirteenth part?
   Ⓐ They thought there would be more than twenty parts.
   Ⓑ They were superstitious.
   Ⓒ They thought it would sink.
   Ⓓ They were afraid of a two-month delay.

13. How will people travel between Denmark and Sweden until the bridge-tunnel is finished?
   Ⓐ by car
   Ⓑ by train
   Ⓒ by ferry
   Ⓓ by bus

14. Why is this bridge-tunnel important to the people of Sweden?
   Ⓐ They're tired of waiting for ferries.
   Ⓑ They like shopping in the capital.
   Ⓒ It has a sunken tube.
   Ⓓ It will connect them to the rest of Europe.

15. What does *sunken* mean in the first paragraph?
   Ⓐ below the surface
   Ⓑ above ground
   Ⓒ circular
   Ⓓ brightly lit

GO ON ⇨

Test 2: Reading Comprehension
(Form A), page 5

Circus elephants have been entertaining audiences for many decades. The most famous elephant of all time was Jumbo. Jumbo was brought to the United States by P.T. Barnum, a world-famous circus owner.

The elephant weighed 12,000 pounds and was over eleven feet tall. When people wanted to describe something very large, they said it was jumbo size. Today we still use that word to describe large items.

Circus elephants are usually female. Trainers say they are easier to work with and train. The female elephants are so gentle that they allow people to ride on their backs. They learn many stunts, such as parading in a line and standing on their hind legs. Elephants are some of the most interesting animals in the circus.

16. Why are circus elephants usually female?
   Ⓐ They like to do stunts.
   Ⓑ They weigh 12,000 pounds.
   Ⓒ They are easier to train.
   Ⓓ They are very interesting.

17. If you buy a *jumbo*-size container of popcorn, it is _____.
   Ⓐ very small
   Ⓑ very large
   Ⓒ average size
   Ⓓ very tiny

18. You can tell from this selection that the author thinks _____.
   Ⓐ elephants are famous
   Ⓑ P.T. Barnum knew a lot about elephants
   Ⓒ all elephants are jumbo size
   Ⓓ elephants are interesting animals

19. What does the word *stunt* mean in this article?
   Ⓐ a description
   Ⓑ a trick
   Ⓒ a circus owner
   Ⓓ a very large animal

GO ON ⇨

Test 2: Reading Comprehension (Form A), page 6

During the War of 1812 when Francis Scott Key wrote "The Star-Spangled Banner," he was being held prisoner by the British. Key was on an assignment from the U.S. government. He was trying to get a prisoner released. The British had burned Washington, D.C., in 1814 and were heading toward Baltimore, but Fort McHenry stood in their way. The British would not let Key leave until after they attacked Fort McHenry. The British fleet fired shells at the fort for a day and a night.

Early the next morning, the smoke and haze from the bombardment made it almost impossible to tell if the fort was still standing. As the dawn grew lighter, onlookers could see the fort still standing. High above the walls of the fort, the tattered ensign was waving. Francis Scott Key was so inspired by the sight of the U.S. flag still flying that he wrote most of his poem in one day. He had it printed the next day. It was set to an Old English tune and was sung as an unofficial anthem for many years. Finally, in 1931 it became the American national anthem.

20. A good title for this selection could be _____.
    Ⓐ How the U.S. Got Its National Anthem
    Ⓑ The History of Fort McHenry
    Ⓒ Flag, Flags, Flags
    Ⓓ All About Francis Scott Key

21. Which happened first?
    Ⓐ The British shelled Fort McHenry.
    Ⓑ Francis Scott Key saw the flag still flying.
    Ⓒ The British burned Washington, D.C.
    Ⓓ There was a lot of smoke and haze.

22. What do the words *tattered ensign* mean in this selection?
    Ⓐ a striped flag
    Ⓑ a torn flag
    Ⓒ a flag that is star-spangled
    Ⓓ a national anthem

23. Why did "The Star-Spangled Banner" become the U.S. national anthem?
    Ⓐ It was sung as an unofficial anthem for over 100 years.
    Ⓑ It was set to an old English tune.
    Ⓒ It was written in one day.
    Ⓓ Fort McHenry was still standing.

GO ON ⇨

24. You can tell that Francis Scott Key was _____.
Ⓐ an obedient prisoner
Ⓑ on the side of the British
Ⓒ very patriotic
Ⓓ wanting to see Fort McHenry destroyed

25. Another word for *bombardment* in this selection is _____.
Ⓐ prisoner
Ⓑ fort
Ⓒ bonfire
Ⓓ attack

Tornadoes, cyclones, earthquakes, and hurricanes create enormous problems for people. The devastation they cause can last for years.

In 1992 Hurricane Andrew became one of the most costly natural disasters in United States history. With winds that reached 164 miles an hour, the storm ruined many towns in its wake. Hardest hit was an area 20–35 miles wide south of Miami.

In addition to the damage Hurricane Andrew did to homes and businesses in that area, water, sewage, and electricity were affected. Food spoiled because there was no refrigeration. Many roads were closed because of the great amount of debris left by the storm. Food, water, medicine, and gasoline were desperately needed but were difficult to deliver. Life was difficult for many people for a long time after Hurricane Andrew finally left.

26. What is the main idea of this selection?
Ⓐ Food should be refrigerated.
Ⓑ Hurricanes can reach 164 miles an hour.
Ⓒ Tornadoes are not as bad as hurricanes.
Ⓓ Hurricanes can cause a great amount of damage.

27. What does the word *devastation* mean in the first paragraph?
Ⓐ destruction
Ⓑ natural
Ⓒ problems
Ⓓ expenses

28. Why was it difficult to deliver the supplies that people needed?
Ⓐ The area was too wide.
Ⓑ The roads were closed.
Ⓒ There was no refrigeration.
Ⓓ Life was difficult.

29. Which would be a good title for this selection?
Ⓐ Hurricane Andrew
Ⓑ Tornadoes and Cyclones
Ⓒ Damage Estimates
Ⓓ Life in Miami

GO ON ⇨

Test 2: Reading Comprehension (Form A), page 8

In ancient Greece, people who had personal problems that they couldn't solve went to the island of Delphi for help. They wanted to get help from the oracle who gave advice from the Greek gods. The wisdom of the Delphi oracle was thought to be supreme, so people from all over Greece made pilgrimages to get advice. What was the oracle's most famous advice? The advice was to "know thyself." This advice didn't really tell the person looking for help how to solve a problem. It only told him to find the answer.

Today, many hundreds of years later, people no longer go to the oracle for help, but they still are trying to find the answers to personal problems. They are discovering that the best way to solve these problems is to start by understanding themselves. Who they are, what their ambitions are, and what really interests them are some of the questions people should ask themselves. The advice given by the Delphi oracle centuries ago is still good today.

30. What does the word *oracle* mean in this article?
   Ⓐ a wise spokesperson for Greek gods
   Ⓑ a Greek island
   Ⓒ good advice
   Ⓓ a supreme person

31. Which of these statements is *not* true?
   Ⓐ Ancient Greeks sought help from the oracle at Delphi.
   Ⓑ "Know thyself" is good advice.
   Ⓒ The oracle is still giving advice today.
   Ⓓ The Delphi oracle gave advice centuries ago.

32. What does the word *pilgrimage* mean in this article?
   Ⓐ a Greek person
   Ⓑ a journey to a special place or shrine
   Ⓒ a way to get advice
   Ⓓ another word for *centuries*

33. Which would be a good title for this selection?
   Ⓐ Going to Delphi
   Ⓑ Finding Personal Problems
   Ⓒ Discovering Islands
   Ⓓ Searching for Advice

GO ON ⇨

Test 2: Reading Comprehension
(Form A), page 9

Modem is a short way of saying *modulator/demodulator*. What is a modem? How does it help you communicate when it is in your computer? When you send an e-mail letter, your modem takes digital information, called *bits*, modulates the bits into analog signals, and then sends the bits over regular phone lines. When you receive e-mail, the modem demodulates the information coming in over the phone lines.

Modems use different tones to represent different bits of data. Each set of tones is called a *symbol*. A baud measures the number of symbols, or discrete units of information expressed by modulation, per second. The measurement is named for Jean-Emile Baudot, a Frenchman who developed a binary code in the 1800s. However, modems weren't widely used until the late 1960s.

Before modems were invented, if people wanted to communicate with each other over computer, the computers had to be "hardwired" together. This was an expensive and complicated process. Modems have made communication cheaper and easier. Without modems we would not have such an easy connection to the Internet that many people use today.

34. What does the word *symbol* mean for modems?
   Ⓐ data demodulation
   Ⓑ communication by telephone
   Ⓒ discrete units of information
   Ⓓ hardwired

35. Which statement is *not* true about this article?
   Ⓐ Bauds are a very recent unit of measurement.
   Ⓑ Bauds were named for Jean-Emile Baudot.
   Ⓒ Modems make it easy to get on the Internet.
   Ⓓ Hardwiring is an expensive process.

36. A good title for this article could be _____.
   Ⓐ Processing Bits
   Ⓑ About Modems
   Ⓒ A Great Frenchman
   Ⓓ Symbols We Use

37. What does *binary* mean in this article?
   Ⓐ a secret
   Ⓑ a number system
   Ⓒ expensive
   Ⓓ yearly

GO ON ⇨

Name _____ Date _____

Test 2: Reading Comprehension
(Form A), page 10

Halley's comet is expected to be visible again in the United States in the year 2062. The comet passes within sight of Earth only once about every 76 years, so most people only get to see it once in their lifetime.

Edmund Halley first saw the comet in 1682. It lit up the night sky for weeks, and many people were afraid that it would never disappear. People were afraid that the comet would come down on Earth and cause the death of many people. Halley tried to tell the public that they had nothing to fear from the comet. He based his belief on his friend Isaac Newton's fairly new scientific theories on gravity. Using these theories, Halley predicted that the comet would return again in the year 1758.

As Halley predicted, the comet returned in 1758. It was Christmas night of that year. Halley died in 1742, so he never knew that his prediction about the comet had come to pass. Because Halley was the person who had made the prediction about the comet's return, people started referring to it as "Halley's Comet."

Because of its shape and the many stories about its sightings, the comet came to be called "The Flaming Sword." Some people started to connect the comet with the reasons for famine, war, and disease. They thought it was an evil star and the bearer of bad news.

38. What kind of person was Halley?
   Ⓐ He was willing to accept new ideas.
   Ⓑ He was not a good predictor of scientific events.
   Ⓒ He liked to look at the Sun.
   Ⓓ He was very famous.

39. How was Halley able to predict the reappearance of the comet?
   Ⓐ He guessed the time based on information he read.
   Ⓑ He was able to count the number of years it had been seen before.
   Ⓒ He applied Newton's theory of gravity to the comet's path.
   Ⓓ He died in 1742.

40. Why was Halley's name given to the comet?
   Ⓐ He first saw the comet in 1682.
   Ⓑ He told people that the comet would not fall to Earth.
   Ⓒ It was considered an evil star.
   Ⓓ He predicted that the comet would reappear in 1758.

41. In what way were Newton and Halley alike?
   Ⓐ They saw the comet at the same time.
   Ⓑ They were good friends.
   Ⓒ They were scientists.
   Ⓓ They knew how to predict wars.

GO ON ⇒

Test 2: Reading Comprehension
(Form A), page 11

Curtain Time

Standing silently among the others
through months of heat, wind, rain,
        and Sun
Your sameness a backdrop
your greenness, soothing,
calming.
Distracted
audiences pass by
immersed in private thoughts

Presently you erupt into color—
        rust, orange, gold,
no longer one of many.
Stepping onto center stage
you bask in your moment
of glory...then
fade into the scenery
and wait silently with the others.

Beatrice G. Davis

42. What season of the year is this
    poem about?
    Ⓐ winter
    Ⓑ spring
    Ⓒ summer
    Ⓓ fall

43. To whom is the poet speaking?
    Ⓐ audiences
    Ⓑ a tree
    Ⓒ heat
    Ⓓ rain

44. Which words tell you that the poet
    thinks of this scene as a stage set?
    Ⓐ wait silently with the others
    Ⓑ no longer one of many
    Ⓒ fade into the scenery
    Ⓓ presently you erupt

45. In this poem the word *immersed*
    means _____.
    Ⓐ born
    Ⓑ torn down
    Ⓒ multiplied by
    Ⓓ involved in

STOP

Test 2: Reading Comprehension (Form B)

Directions For questions 1–43 read each selection. Then answer each question about the selection.

Sample

A long line of covered vehicles drawn by slow, plodding oxen drew closer. Beside the wagons, armed men walked cautiously. Inside the wagons were women, children, furniture, and supplies. In the rear was a guard of six men. This was the famous wagon train.

1. What kind of vehicles is the author describing?
   - Ⓐ trucks
   - Ⓑ vans
   - Ⓒ covered wagons
   - Ⓓ trailers

2. Why were the men walking cautiously?
   - Ⓐ They were afraid of attacks.
   - Ⓑ They didn't want to disturb the women and children.
   - Ⓒ The oxen were moving very slowly.
   - Ⓓ They wanted to keep up with the men in the rear.

Time: 45 minutes

Some people have dangerous occupations. One of the most dangerous occupations is sponge diving. Sponges are springy, porous masses of fibers that form the skeletons of certain underwater species that live in warm seas.

The divers leap into uncertain waters wearing no protective clothing or equipment. Man-eating fish lurk on all sides. Even the strongest swimmers are sometimes carried off course by undertows. There are also heavy, tangled undersea growths. Divers are often trapped here as they search for the best sponges. Sponge diving is especially risky.

1. What does the word *lurk* mean in paragraph 2?
   - Ⓐ move around secretly
   - Ⓑ play games
   - Ⓒ eat lunch
   - Ⓓ swim backward

GO ON ⇨

Test 2: Reading Comprehension (Form B), page 2

2. What does the author mean by "uncertain waters"?
   Ⓐ Not all of the water is warm.
   Ⓑ There is no safety equipment.
   Ⓒ There are many dangerous occupations.
   Ⓓ The water has many dangers for divers.

3. Why could the divers get trapped in the undersea growths?
   Ⓐ The man-eating fish are lurking on all sides.
   Ⓑ They are looking for the best sponges.
   Ⓒ They are not wearing protective clothing.
   Ⓓ The waters are uncertain.

4. How does the author prove that sponge diving is dangerous?
   Ⓐ He says there are many dangerous occupations.
   Ⓑ He thinks that sponge diving is especially risky.
   Ⓒ He describes three hazards that make sponge diving risky.
   Ⓓ He thinks the divers take too many chances.

The most important thing to remember is not to worry. You can't do your best thinking if you worry about the possibility of failing. The next important thing to remember is to divide your time properly. If you spend too much time on one question, you might not have time to finish the entire test. Above all, carefully read the directions. Many students have tested poorly because they failed to take the time to understand the directions and questions.

5. A good title for this paragraph could be _____.
   Ⓐ How to Do Your Best Thinking
   Ⓑ How to Divide Your Time
   Ⓒ How to Take a Test
   Ⓓ How to Understand Questions

6. What does the author say is the second most important thing to remember when taking a test?
   Ⓐ Don't worry.
   Ⓑ Divide your time properly.
   Ⓒ Understand the questions and directions.
   Ⓓ Finish the entire test.

GO ON ⇨

Test 2: Reading Comprehension
(Form B), page 3

7. Why is it important to divide your time properly?
- Ⓐ so you can understand the directions
- Ⓑ so you won't have to worry
- Ⓒ so you won't be afraid
- Ⓓ so you'll have time to finish the test

8. How does the author prove that it is important to understand the directions and questions?
- Ⓐ She tells you not to worry.
- Ⓑ She says many have done poorly because they didn't understand the questions.
- Ⓒ She tells you how to divide your time properly.
- Ⓓ She tells you about the possibility of failing.

Jove, a Greek god, had many sons. He was thought of as being cheerful and hearty. Today when we describe someone as being cheerful, we say that person is very *jovial*. Jove also had a sister named Ceres. She was the goddess of agriculture. The word *cereal* comes from her name.

Mars is the name of a planet and of a famous son of the Greek god Jove. Mars is the god of war, so when we speak of military things, we often use the word *martial*. When we talk about people who might live on the planet Mars, we call them *Martians*. The month of March is named for Mars.

January is named for Janus, another son of Jove. Janus had two faces, one in front, looking ahead, and one in back, looking to the past. Perhaps the month of January was named for Janus because it comes after the old year and at the beginning of the new year.

Another son of Jove was Mercury. Mercury is the name of the metallic element Hg, the only liquid metal. Mercury is also the name of a planet. Mercury was a very speedy messenger when he delivered the messages of the Greek gods. The messages were always delivered to different places or positions in time. When we speak of people who move about quickly and are always changing, we call them *mercurial*.

Pan was the Greek god of the woods and forests. He is usually shown as being half man and half goat. It was believed that Pan lived in places where people did not go. Sometimes when people are alone in nature or new situations, they become frightened. The word used to describe this feeling is *panic* or *panicky*.

9. What is the main idea of this selection?
- Ⓐ to tell about Jove and his sons
- Ⓑ to tell about planets that are named for Greek gods
- Ⓒ to tell how some words became part of our language
- Ⓓ to teach us more about Greek mythology

GO ON ⇨

Name _____   Date _____

Test 2: Reading Comprehension
(Form B), page 4

10. The metal Mercury is also called quicksilver. How is the god Mercury like the metal Mercury?
   Ⓐ He doesn't stay in the same place long.
   Ⓑ He is Jove's son.
   Ⓒ He has a famous brother.
   Ⓓ He likes to deliver messages.

11. Why does the author compare the god Janus to the month of January?
   Ⓐ January is a cold month.
   Ⓑ January faces the old and the new.
   Ⓒ Janus was a good son.
   Ⓓ Janus was the brother of Mars.

12. Which of these is an opinion?
   Ⓐ Many of our words come from Greek gods.
   Ⓑ Jove had many sons.
   Ⓒ Mercury is the name of a planet.
   Ⓓ Pan was Jove's favorite son.

13. Which of these could be a title for this article?
   Ⓐ Words We Get from Greek Mythology
   Ⓑ Jove and His Sons
   Ⓒ Greek Gods and Their Planets
   Ⓓ The Martians Are Coming

14. If someone you know likes to have fun, you might say that person is most like _____.
   Ⓐ Janus
   Ⓑ Pan
   Ⓒ Mars
   Ⓓ Jove

15. What can you conclude about the author of this article?
   Ⓐ He believes you should always use the dictionary.
   Ⓑ He believes that everyone should study mythology.
   Ⓒ He is interested in studying the origin of words.
   Ⓓ He knows a lot about the planets.

GO ON ⇨

Test 2: Reading Comprehension (Form B), page 5

The telephone, which was a novelty in 1877, soon caught on with amazing speed. Because direct dialing had not been invented yet, all calls were placed by an operator. The first operators were young men, but they were soon replaced by young women. The telephone company believed that women's voices and personalities were better suited to the job. Because "Central," as the operators were called, could listen in on every conversation they placed, companies had strict rules about operators who might give out information about phone calls they heard. There were large fines and threats of imprisonment for anyone who broke these rules.

Early in the twentieth century, telephones were in such common use that it was hard to imagine how we ever got along without them. What would users of those early phones think if they saw us using cell phones in cars and phones so small they fit in our pocket?

16. How many years has it been since phones became popular?
   Ⓐ more than 200 years
   Ⓑ about 120 years
   Ⓒ less than 100 years
   Ⓓ about 150 years

17. Why did phone companies have rules about listening in on conversations?
   Ⓐ They wanted to protect their customers' privacy.
   Ⓑ They wanted to protect "Central" operators.
   Ⓒ They thought that women liked to be fined.
   Ⓓ They could charge more money for use of phones.

18. Where do you think the author may have found the information for this article?
   Ⓐ an atlas
   Ⓑ an encyclopedia
   Ⓒ a dictionary
   Ⓓ a thesaurus

19. The word *novelty* in this selection means _____.
   Ⓐ an ice-cream cone
   Ⓑ a high-pitched voice
   Ⓒ a large fine
   Ⓓ a new, unusual item

GO ON ⇨

Name _____   Date _____

Test 2: Reading Comprehension
(Form B), page 6

The American Red Cross was a very new organization in 1889. In June of that year, the organization founded by Clara Barton had its first test—to help the survivors of the great Johnstown Flood.

Clara Barton was described as a stiff-spined little woman wearing muddy boots when she arrived in Johnstown with a group of fifty men and women to see what help was needed. Barton had been through two wars. She was five feet tall and, although she was sixty-seven years old, she did not have a gray hair on her head. Clara Barton seemed to require very little sleep and was what we would today call a "workaholic." She had no use for anyone who tried to tell her how to run her business.

Clara Barton set up headquarters inside an abandoned railroad car. She used a packing box for a desk. She worked almost around the clock, directing hundreds of volunteers, distributing blankets, clothing, food, and half a million dollars. Temporary housing was put up according to her orders. She ordered a Red Cross "hospital" to be set up.

Barton stayed on the scene for five months. When she left she received many blessings and thanks. Newspapers wrote glowing editorials about her. She was given a diamond-studded locket. In Washington, D.C., President and Mrs. Harrison attended a dinner in her honor. The American Red Cross clearly had arrived!

20. In what year did the Johnstown Flood happen?
    Ⓐ 1900
    Ⓑ 1899
    Ⓒ 1889
    Ⓓ 1890

21. Why was Barton described as being stiff-spined?
    Ⓐ She was very tall.
    Ⓑ She stood up straight.
    Ⓒ She gave a lot of help.
    Ⓓ She did not allow any nonsense.

22. What was surprising about her appearance?
    Ⓐ She was five feet tall.
    Ⓑ She did not have gray hair.
    Ⓒ She did not need much sleep.
    Ⓓ She had been through two wars.

GO ON ⇨

Test 2: Reading Comprehension
(Form B), page 7

23. What does the word *temporary* mean in this article?
Ⓐ not permanent
Ⓑ reliable
Ⓒ careless
Ⓓ long-standing

24. How did Barton know that the American Red Cross had finally arrived?
Ⓐ Everyone thanked her.
Ⓑ She worked for five months.
Ⓒ She distributed half a million dollars.
Ⓓ President Harrison and his wife attended a dinner in her honor.

25. What does *abandoned* mean in this selection?
Ⓐ unpainted
Ⓑ modern
Ⓒ deserted
Ⓓ an office

How To Make a Relief Map

First, find a map that you can use to trace the outline for whatever state or country you are studying. This will give you an idea of the size and shape your map will be. Next, find a heavy piece of cardboard or some other sturdy material to use as a base.

After you get the base, cut out the map you want to use and trace its outline on the base. Now comes the fun part. Make salt dough to cover the outline you have drawn on the base. For the salt dough, you will need 2 cups of flour, 1 cup of coarse salt, and 1 cup of water. Use a wooden spoon to mix the flour and salt in a flat-bottomed pan. Gradually add small amounts of water. Continue to stir and add water until the mixture looks like dough. Knead the dough for about seven or eight minutes until you can form a smooth, firm ball.

If you plan to use the dough later, put it in a plastic bag or plastic wrap. When you are ready to use the dough, lightly flour your hands and the surface you will be working on. Roll out the dough and press it into the shape you need. If you want to add pieces to change the shape, moisten the pieces and press them together.

Bake the dough in a 325 to 350 degree oven until it is light golden-brown. If you are not allowed to use the oven, air-drying the dough works just as well. Just leave it out in the air for 48 hours. When it is ready, you can paint the different areas of the map according to the features you want to show.

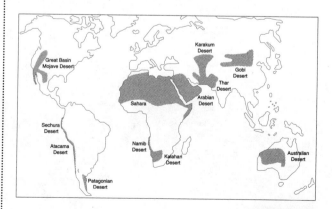

GO ON ⇨

Test 2: Reading Comprehension
(Form B), page 8

26. What does the author think about making salt dough?
- Ⓐ It is messy.
- Ⓑ It is hard work.
- Ⓒ It should always be baked.
- Ⓓ It is fun.

27. What should you do after you have chosen a base?
- Ⓐ Trace the outline of your map onto the base.
- Ⓑ Start to make the salt dough.
- Ⓒ Find a map you can use.
- Ⓓ Find a flat-bottomed pan.

28. How can you show different features on your map?
- Ⓐ Knead the dough for 7–8 minutes.
- Ⓑ Use two cups of flour.
- Ⓒ Paint the dough in different colors.
- Ⓓ Let the dough air-dry.

29. Why should you put the dough in a plastic bag or wrap?
- Ⓐ It will stay moist until you are ready to use it.
- Ⓑ You will be able to bake it.
- Ⓒ It will fit on the base.
- Ⓓ You can add pieces to change the shape.

Researchers have discovered that the big, brown bats from New England may be useful for improving the accuracy of sonar that the Navy uses to locate mines and submarines. The improvements in sonar could also help a design team at the University of Texas to work on developing a smart, motorized wheelchair capable of following voice commands. People in wheelchairs would have more freedom to move around, because they could use the sonar to tell them when they were approaching an obstacle and move to avoid it.

One of the problems of making a smart wheelchair is that many insurance companies won't pay for the high cost of such a wheelchair. However, signals that come from more inexpensive sonar devices bounce in such a way that they give the appearance of an opening in a wall even when there isn't one. Inexpensive devices also have trouble recognizing glass and the vertical drop-off from a curb or stairwell.

The bat sonar findings may solve some of these problems. Scientists have found that the dime-sized brains of these big, brown bats can sense overlapping echoes three times faster and better than the best Navy equipment. This ability will make a useful computer model for designing software to improve Navy sonar. Hopefully, the cost of a smart wheelchair will decrease, too.

GO ON ⇨

Test 2: Reading Comprehension
(Form B), page 9

30. What does the Navy use sonar equipment for?
    Ⓐ to do research with bats
    Ⓑ to locate mines and submarines
    Ⓒ to build wheelchairs
    Ⓓ to bounce signals off walls

31. Why would sonar equipment based on the bat computer model help people in wheelchairs?
    Ⓐ They could control the wheelchair's movement with their voice.
    Ⓑ They could sense overlapping echoes.
    Ⓒ The costs would be very high.
    Ⓓ They don't recognize glass.

32. What would make a wheelchair smart?
    Ⓐ if it improved the accuracy of sonar
    Ⓑ if it could be motorized
    Ⓒ if it followed voice commands
    Ⓓ if the Navy could use it

33. What does the word *obstacle* mean in this article?
    Ⓐ a bat
    Ⓑ a loud signal
    Ⓒ something in the way of
    Ⓓ a voice command

It is this player's duty to keep the opposing team from scoring. He or she must get the bunts and try to pick off runners on bases. Of great importance is this player's ability to substitute for an infielder who was forced to leave his or her position. If this player happens to be a good batter too, he or she is even more valuable.

34. What team position is described in this paragraph?
    Ⓐ catcher
    Ⓑ shortstop
    Ⓒ pitcher
    Ⓓ umpire

35. Why is it important to get the bunts?
    Ⓐ to be a good batter
    Ⓑ to pick off runners on bases
    Ⓒ to substitute for an infielder
    Ⓓ to be a good catcher

GO ON ⇨

Test 2: Reading Comprehension
(Form B), page 10

In the early 1900s, most people thought that female photographers should do fashion photography or portraits. Margaret Bourke-White did not agree. She was determined to do what she considered more serious photography. She wanted to photograph the events of the world of her time. She started by taking pictures of the skylines of great cities. In her search for new angles from which to take pictures, she frequently found herself in very dangerous positions. The pictures she got as a result of being so daring were judged extraordinary.

When photojournalism, telling a story with a series of pictures, became popular, Margaret Bourke-White soon became a leader in this kind of photography. Her picture stories about Russia in the 1930s were published in two books. In 1933 she was hired by *Life* magazine. This magazine was the first picture newsmagazine. Bourke-White took the cover picture for the first issue and remained a star photographer/reporter for *Life* for over thirty years.

During World War II, under direct orders from General Eisenhower, Margaret was flown to every combat zone. She covered all the major battles and every important person in them. She went anywhere she thought there might be a good picture or story. As you can imagine, Margaret had many close calls while working to get the pictures that she thought were needed to make a good photo-news story. Today, photographers who work for photo newsmagazines, such as *People,* may not know it, but they have Margaret Bourke-White to thank for leading the way in this field.

36. What made Margaret Bourke-White's photographs unusual?
    Ⓐ They were pictures of skylines.
    Ⓑ They were taken from surprising angles.
    Ⓒ They were important to Margaret.
    Ⓓ They were pictures of the world.

GO ON ⇨

Test 2: Reading Comprehension
(Form B), page 11

37. How was *Life* magazine different from other magazines of the 1930s?
  (A) It had pictures of Russia.
  (B) It featured fashion photography.
  (C) It was a natural place for a woman photographer.
  (D) It was the first picture newsmagazine.

38. What does the author think of Margaret Bourke-White?
  (A) She was an outstanding photographer.
  (B) Her pictures weren't very interesting.
  (C) She should have stayed home during World War II.
  (D) She was a good writer.

39. What is a *close call*?
  (A) a local phone call
  (B) a nearby voice
  (C) a new angle
  (D) a narrow escape from danger

Chengwena Faces the Future

dusty settlement
treeless plain
clusters of thatch-roofed rondavels
simple community structures ...
this is the village of Chengwena

smiling, barefoot children
wearing faded school uniforms
women garbed in colorful tribal dress
men in business-like suits and ties
greet us, say "welcome"...
these are the people of Chengwena

we are here to celebrate
how the gift of a welding machine
has brought great joy and pride
to their village
the welder demonstrates his skills
shows how he repairs scotch carts
makes window bars, wrought
     iron chairs
tells how he guards this treasure
in a hut where he sleeps by its side...
this is the spirit of Chengwena

we exchange speeches
are entertained with song and dance
given gifts of pumpkins and
     ground nuts
feasted with chicken and rice
which we eat with our fingers

as my world hurtles on the
superhighway to a new millennium
this is Chengwena...inching along

Beatrice G. Davis

GO ON ⇨

Test 2: Reading Comprehension
(Form B), page 12

40. Where do you think the village of Chengwena is located?

Ⓐ United States

Ⓑ France

Ⓒ Africa

Ⓓ Canada

41. What are the people of the village celebrating?

Ⓐ the superhighway

Ⓑ a welding machine

Ⓒ scotch carts

Ⓓ singing and dancing

42. Why does the welder sleep in the hut with the welding machine?

Ⓐ He wants to guard it.

Ⓑ He has no other place to sleep.

Ⓒ He wants to make chairs.

Ⓓ He wants to make a speech.

43. Why does the poet say that Chengwena is inching along?

Ⓐ They don't have modern conveniences.

Ⓑ They have a welding machine.

Ⓒ They make good feasts.

Ⓓ The children are barefoot.

STOP

STOP

Test 3: Language Mechanics/Spelling (Form A)

Directions For questions 1–10 darken the circle for the word that is spelled correctly.

Sample A

A _____ was sighted near our city.
- Ⓐ tornaido
- Ⓑ tornado
- Ⓒ tornadow
- Ⓓ ternado

Time: 15 minutes

1. I write in my _____ daily.
   - Ⓐ journal
   - Ⓑ jernal
   - Ⓒ jurnel
   - Ⓓ journale

2. A shooting star is really a _____.
   - Ⓐ meateor
   - Ⓑ meeteor
   - Ⓒ meteeor
   - Ⓓ meteor

3. Please _____ the camera sharply.
   - Ⓐ fockus
   - Ⓑ focus
   - Ⓒ fowcus
   - Ⓓ fohcus

4. Joe is a _____ in high school.
   - Ⓐ senior
   - Ⓑ senoir
   - Ⓒ seenyur
   - Ⓓ seanor

5. To find the sum, use _____.
   - Ⓐ additon
   - Ⓑ addition
   - Ⓒ adition
   - Ⓓ additsion

6. To find the difference, use _____.
   - Ⓐ subtration
   - Ⓑ subtrackion
   - Ⓒ subtracton
   - Ⓓ subtraction

7. A huge _____ fell onto the road.
   - Ⓐ boldre
   - Ⓑ bowlder
   - Ⓒ boulder
   - Ⓓ bolour

8. I _____ you to do your best.
   - Ⓐ encourage
   - Ⓑ incourage
   - Ⓒ encurage
   - Ⓓ encourige

9. Her _____ birthday is today.
   - Ⓐ twintieth
   - Ⓑ twenteuth
   - Ⓒ twentieth
   - Ⓓ twentyth

10. Use logic to draw a _____.
    - Ⓐ concloosion
    - Ⓑ cunclusion
    - Ⓒ conclusion
    - Ⓓ concluzion

GO ON ⇨

Test 3: Language Mechanics/Spelling (Form A), page 2

Directions For questions 11–20 darken the circle for the letter of the phrase that has a misspelled underlined word.

Sample B

(A) pint of <u>barbecue</u>

(B) <u>quort</u> of milk

(C) cup of <u>liquid</u>

(D) gallon of <u>cider</u>

---

11. (A) character's <u>role</u>
    (B) actors' <u>costumes</u>
    (C) <u>reherse</u> the play
    (D) <u>audience</u> laughter

12. (A) <u>acheve</u> a goal
    (B) <u>absorb</u> information
    (C) <u>bustle</u> around
    (D) <u>concentrate</u> well

13. (A) a brief <u>bullitin</u>
    (B) a <u>gourmet</u> restaurant
    (C) an <u>elegant</u> occasion
    (D) a <u>pinkish</u> grapefruit

14. (A) <u>sensible</u> idea
    (B) <u>dependible</u> employee
    (C) <u>gigantic</u> project
    (D) <u>shrewd</u> advice

15. (A) a deep <u>cavurn</u>
    (B) a shiny <u>emerald</u>
    (C) a <u>casual</u> dinner
    (D) a <u>fragrant</u> flower

16. (A) chemical <u>compound</u>
    (B) law of <u>gravity</u>
    (C) the <u>soler</u> system
    (D) <u>lowland</u> stream

17. (A) <u>scaly</u> trout
    (B) weary <u>straggler</u>
    (C) <u>troublesome</u> traffic
    (D) <u>wintery</u> weather

18. (A) outdated <u>atlus</u>
    (B) <u>humorous</u> comment
    (C) <u>realistic</u> outlook
    (D) <u>positive</u> attitude

19. (A) steady <u>rainfall</u>
    (B) famous <u>patriot</u>
    (C) <u>reckless</u> youth
    (D) well-known <u>commet</u>

20. (A) a <u>poisionous</u> snake
    (B) a <u>hideous</u> mess
    (C) a <u>murky</u> sea
    (D) a <u>truthful</u> answer

STOP

STOP

Test 3: Language Mechanics/Usage (Form A)

Directions For questions 1–10 darken the circle for the word or words that best complete each sentence.

Sample A

I ran _____ of all.
- Ⓐ fastest
- Ⓑ faster
- Ⓒ fast
- Ⓓ more fast

Time: 28 minutes

1. We ate _____ to enjoy the meal.
   - Ⓐ slower
   - Ⓑ slow
   - Ⓒ slowly
   - Ⓓ slowed

2. Anne had _____ the play before.
   - Ⓐ saw
   - Ⓑ seen
   - Ⓒ seed
   - Ⓓ see

3. They _____ hoping to buy a house.
   - Ⓐ was
   - Ⓑ were
   - Ⓒ is
   - Ⓓ wasn't

4. Most people _____ of Benjamin Franklin before.
   - Ⓐ has heard
   - Ⓑ hearing
   - Ⓒ have heard
   - Ⓓ was heard

5. John _____ his homework.
   - Ⓐ done
   - Ⓑ do
   - Ⓒ has did
   - Ⓓ did

6. Jesse asked _____ to meet him.
   - Ⓐ us
   - Ⓑ we
   - Ⓒ their
   - Ⓓ our

7. _____ dog is friendly to me.
   - Ⓐ You're
   - Ⓑ Yours
   - Ⓒ Your
   - Ⓓ Yore

8. My dad is a _____ cook.
   - Ⓐ goodest
   - Ⓑ best
   - Ⓒ well
   - Ⓓ good

9. Next week I _____ to the beach.
   - Ⓐ went
   - Ⓑ have gone
   - Ⓒ will go
   - Ⓓ going

10. Mom told _____ to come home.
    - Ⓐ him
    - Ⓑ he
    - Ⓒ his
    - Ⓓ he's

GO ON ⇨

Test 3: Language Mechanics/Usage
(Form A), page 2

Directions For questions 11–20 darken the circle for the phrase in each sentence that shows the complete subject or the complete predicate.

Sample B
What is the complete subject of this sentence?
The dog named Rascal ran after a ball.
Ⓐ The dog
Ⓑ Rascal
Ⓒ The dog named Rascal
Ⓓ Rascal ran

11. **What is the complete predicate of this sentence?**
Ralph and Jane got married in June.
Ⓐ Ralph and Jane
Ⓑ got married in June
Ⓒ in June
Ⓓ got married

12. **What is the complete subject of this sentence?**
My younger sister Janet plays softball.
Ⓐ My younger sister
Ⓑ plays softball
Ⓒ My younger sister Janet
Ⓓ Janet plays

13. **What is the complete predicate of this sentence?**
Joel typed and printed his letter.
Ⓐ Joel typed
Ⓑ typed and printed his letter
Ⓒ printed his letter
Ⓓ Joel typed and printed

14. **What is the complete subject of this sentence?**
Mei Lee and several other students wrote the report.
Ⓐ Mei Lee and several other students
Ⓑ wrote the report
Ⓒ several other students
Ⓓ Mei Lee

15. **What is the complete predicate of this sentence?**
Mom and Dad cooked and washed the dishes.
Ⓐ Mom and Dad
Ⓑ cooked and washed
Ⓒ washed the dishes
Ⓓ cooked and washed the dishes

16. **What is the complete subject of this sentence?**
The planet Mercury doesn't have any moons.
Ⓐ Mercury
Ⓑ doesn't have any moons
Ⓒ The planet Mercury
Ⓓ Mercury doesn't have

17. **What is the complete predicate of this sentence?**
The crowd clapped their hands for the winning racer.
Ⓐ clapped their hands for the winning racer
Ⓑ The crowd
Ⓒ crowd clapped
Ⓓ clapped their hands

GO ON ⇨

Test 3: Language Mechanics/Usage (Form A), page 3

18. What is the complete subject of this sentence?

A red sky at sunset means good weather.

- Ⓐ means good weather
- Ⓑ A red sky
- Ⓒ good weather
- Ⓓ A red sky at sunset

19. What is the complete predicate of this sentence?

We don't know where to buy buttons.

- Ⓐ We
- Ⓑ don't know where to buy buttons
- Ⓒ We don't know
- Ⓓ buy buttons

20. What is the complete subject of this sentence?

Running the mile is his favorite race.

- Ⓐ Running
- Ⓑ is his favorite race
- Ⓒ Running the mile
- Ⓓ his favorite race

Directions For questions 21–28 darken the circle for the sentence that shows correct capitalization and punctuation.

Sample C
- Ⓐ Have you had breakfast.
- Ⓑ Where is the leftover pizza?
- Ⓒ Johns father took him to school.
- Ⓓ I play soccer on saturdays.

21.
- Ⓐ Fred wrote a story called "the three thieves."
- Ⓑ I could'nt see in the dark.
- Ⓒ Carol asked, "When is Thanksgiving?"
- Ⓓ Many tourists from america go to Toronto.

22.
- Ⓐ Our class had mayor Davis as a guest speaker.
- Ⓑ Can you come over for dinner.
- Ⓒ The puppies were born on April 5 1998.
- Ⓓ Yes, I'd like to come to the party.

23.
- Ⓐ When I eat breakfast, I feel better at school.
- Ⓑ We made a salad with lettuce tomatoes and celery.
- Ⓒ Detroit Michigan is known for making cars.
- Ⓓ Mr. James McNutt, jr. is my neighbor.

24.
- Ⓐ Get a doctors opinion about your illness.
- Ⓑ Raise your hand to speak please.
- Ⓒ I live on Little Thicket Road.
- Ⓓ Watch out for cars

25.
- Ⓐ Will you help me asked Chris.
- Ⓑ Why did you leave school early?
- Ⓒ We like to eat chinese food for dinner.
- Ⓓ "Linda did you go to school?" he asked.

GO ON ⇨

Test 3: Language Mechanics/Usage (Form A), page 4

26. Ⓐ Everyones ideas are worth hearing.
    Ⓑ We saw rabbits, and squirrels in the park.
    Ⓒ This is the best news!
    Ⓓ I heard mrs. Boxer's speech on TV.

27. Ⓐ We spent the day hiking fishing and camping.
    Ⓑ Their two children's rooms are small.
    Ⓒ "Oh did you win the grand prize?" asked Tim.
    Ⓓ It was too rainy, to go for a long walk.

28. Ⓐ No I don't have any money left.
    Ⓑ What an exciting football game that was?
    Ⓒ I like to read poetry by japanese poets.
    Ⓓ June, July, and August are summer months.

Directions For questions 29–33 darken the circle for the choice that shows the correct capitalization and punctuation for the underlined part of each sentence. Darken the circle for *Correct as it is* if there is no error.

Sample D

I am ten, but my brother is eleven.
Ⓐ ten but
Ⓑ ten but,
Ⓒ , ten but
Ⓓ Correct as it is

---

29. Before we leave for school let's make sandwiches.
    Ⓐ school, let's
    Ⓑ , school let's
    Ⓒ school; let's
    Ⓓ Correct as it is

30. People in the flood need food blankets and clothes.
    Ⓐ need, food, blankets and clothes.
    Ⓑ need food, blankets, and clothes.
    Ⓒ need food blankets, and clothes.
    Ⓓ Correct as it is

31. They built a sturdy, brick, two-story house.
    Ⓐ sturdy brick two-story
    Ⓑ sturdy brick, two-story
    Ⓒ , sturdy brick two-story
    Ⓓ Correct as it is

32. The new century begins on Saturday January 1 2000.
    Ⓐ Saturday, January 1 2000.
    Ⓑ Saturday January 1, 2000.
    Ⓒ Saturday, January 1, 2000.
    Ⓓ Correct as it is

33. Ms. Smith, the teacher's aide, called the roll.
    Ⓐ Smith the teacher's aide called
    Ⓑ Smith "the teacher's aide" called
    Ⓒ Smith; the teacher's aide called
    Ⓓ Correct as it is

STOP

Test 4: Language Expression (Form A)

Directions For questions 1–6 darken the circle for the sentence that best combines the underlined sentences.

Sample A

My dog was eating.
She was on the front porch.

Ⓐ My dog she was eating on the front porch.

Ⓑ On the front porch, my dog was eating.

Ⓒ My dog was eating on the front porch.

Ⓓ On the front porch was my dog who was eating.

Time: 15 minutes

1. We had a family party.
   The party was on my birthday.
   Ⓐ On my birthday a family party was had.
   Ⓑ A family party was had on my birthday.
   Ⓒ We had a family party on my birthday.
   Ⓓ On my birthday was had a family party.

2. I rode in my uncle's car.
   The car was new.
   Ⓐ I rode in my uncle's new car.
   Ⓑ I rode in the car of my uncle.
   Ⓒ My uncle's new car I rode in.
   Ⓓ My uncle's new car was ridden in by me.

3. Venus is similar to Earth.
   Venus is hotter than Earth.
   Ⓐ Venus is not similar or hotter than Earth.
   Ⓑ Earth is less hot and similar than Venus.
   Ⓒ Venus is similar to Earth, but it is hotter.
   Ⓓ Venus and Earth are similar but hot.

4. Three pies are on the stove.
   The pies are made of pumpkin.
   Ⓐ On the stove are three pies they are made of pumpkin.
   Ⓑ The three pies on the stove they are made of pumpkin.
   Ⓒ On the stove are the three pies and they are made of pumpkin.
   Ⓓ The three pies on the stove are made of pumpkin.

5. Where is the stamp?
   I asked you to put it on the letter.
   Ⓐ The stamp that I asked you to put on the letter, where is it?
   Ⓑ Where is the stamp that I asked you to put on the letter?
   Ⓒ Where is it, the stamp that I asked you to put on the letter?
   Ⓓ The stamp that I asked you to put it on the letter is where?

GO ON ⇨

Test 4: Language Expression (Form A), page 2

6. <u>I enjoy good comedy.</u>
   <u>I go to a lot of movies.</u>
   Ⓐ I go to a lot of movies so I like good comedy.
   Ⓑ I like good comedy, so I go to a lot of movies.
   Ⓒ Good comedy is what I like at a lot of movies.
   Ⓓ I like good comedy so that to a lot of movies I go.

Directions For questions 7–12 read the selection. Then darken the circle for the correct answer to each question.

The best way to explore is to go hiking. [1] Going hiking on foot is fun. [2] You bring only what you can carry on your back. [3] Before you go, gather some basic gear. [4] You'll need comfortable shoes or boots. [5] Carry a waterproof poncho. [6] Then you'll be prepared for rain. [7] Take some energy bars and a bottle of water? [8] Put all your gear into a backpack also take a compass so you won't get lost. [9] Frank hiked ten miles in one day. [10]

7. Which is the topic sentence?
   Ⓐ Sentence 5
   Ⓑ Sentence 1
   Ⓒ Sentence 4
   Ⓓ Sentence 8

8. Which sentence doesn't belong in the paragraph?
   Ⓐ Sentence 6
   Ⓑ Sentence 10
   Ⓒ Sentence 4
   Ⓓ Sentence 7

9. Which is a run-on sentence?
   Ⓐ Sentence 9
   Ⓑ Sentence 8
   Ⓒ Sentence 7
   Ⓓ Sentence 6

10. Which sentences could be combined?
   Ⓐ Sentences 1 and 2
   Ⓑ Sentences 6 and 7
   Ⓒ Sentences 8 and 9
   Ⓓ None of them

11. Which sentence has incorrect punctuation?
   Ⓐ Sentence 2
   Ⓑ Sentence 4
   Ⓒ Sentence 8
   Ⓓ Sentence 10

12. Which sentences have compound words?
   Ⓐ Sentences 1 and 6
   Ⓑ Sentences 2 and 3
   Ⓒ Sentences 8 and 9
   Ⓓ Sentences 6 and 9

STOP

Test 3: Language Mechanics/Spelling (Form B)

Directions For questions 1–10 darken the circle for the word that is spelled correctly.

Sample A

There is more than one _____ of how the solar system was formed.
- Ⓐ theary
- Ⓑ threory
- Ⓒ theery
- Ⓓ theory

Time: 15 minutes

1. I finished my homework _____.
   - Ⓐ assignment
   - Ⓑ asignment
   - Ⓒ assighment
   - Ⓓ assinement

2. The force that pulls things toward Earth is _____.
   - Ⓐ grahvity
   - Ⓑ grauvity
   - Ⓒ gravity
   - Ⓓ graovity

3. I saw heavy _____ in the factory.
   - Ⓐ mashinery
   - Ⓑ machinery
   - Ⓒ mahchinery
   - Ⓓ machinary

4. The Moon is a _____ of the Earth.
   - Ⓐ satelite
   - Ⓑ satilight
   - Ⓒ satellite
   - Ⓓ satalite

5. Dinosaurs are _____ animals.
   - Ⓐ prehistoric
   - Ⓑ prehystoric
   - Ⓒ prehistoryic
   - Ⓓ prehisstoric

6. Mrs. Smith is a state _____.
   - Ⓐ senitor
   - Ⓑ cenitor
   - Ⓒ senator
   - Ⓓ sennator

7. My _____ needs a new battery.
   - Ⓐ wristwach
   - Ⓑ wrestwatch
   - Ⓒ ristwatch
   - Ⓓ wristwatch

8. We have a _____ teacher today.
   - Ⓐ substatute
   - Ⓑ substitute
   - Ⓒ substitoot
   - Ⓓ subsitute

9. Geometry is a kind of _____.
   - Ⓐ mathemaitics
   - Ⓑ mathamatics
   - Ⓒ mathematics
   - Ⓓ mathmatics

10. Another word for *doctor* is _____.
    - Ⓐ fisitian
    - Ⓑ physician
    - Ⓒ physitian
    - Ⓓ phisitian

GO ON ⇨

Test 3: Language Mechanics/Spelling (Form B), page 2

Directions For questions 11–20 darken the circle for the letter of the phrase that has a misspelled underlined word.

Sample B
- Ⓐ pain and <u>againy</u>
- Ⓑ zany <u>zebra</u>
- Ⓒ <u>spaghetti</u> and meatballs
- Ⓓ <u>unknown</u> person

11. Ⓐ <u>agreeable</u> person
    Ⓑ medical <u>reserch</u>
    Ⓒ loud <u>announcer</u>
    Ⓓ summer <u>recess</u>

12. Ⓐ doctor's <u>office</u>
    Ⓑ <u>routeen</u> checkup
    Ⓒ <u>nurse's</u> aide
    Ⓓ <u>battery</u> of tests

13. Ⓐ <u>distant</u> lands
    Ⓑ <u>invisible</u> tape
    Ⓒ birthday <u>celabration</u>
    Ⓓ dental <u>appointment</u>

14. Ⓐ <u>popular</u> movie
    Ⓑ <u>unusual</u> question
    Ⓒ <u>interesting</u> book
    Ⓓ <u>sinsere</u> apology

15. Ⓐ Earth's <u>atmosphear</u>
    Ⓑ rainy <u>forecast</u>
    Ⓒ <u>ancient</u> times
    Ⓓ <u>bouncing</u> rays

16. Ⓐ <u>nonfiction</u> book
    Ⓑ recent <u>biograpy</u>
    Ⓒ fictional <u>character</u>
    Ⓓ <u>library</u> book

17. Ⓐ mass <u>transit</u>
    Ⓑ traffic <u>calming</u>
    Ⓒ <u>community</u> center
    Ⓓ neighborhood <u>assiociation</u>

18. Ⓐ <u>wildflower</u> center
    Ⓑ <u>refrence</u> book
    Ⓒ <u>textbook</u> committee
    Ⓓ <u>sculpture</u> garden

19. Ⓐ safe <u>enviroment</u>
    Ⓑ foggy <u>ridge</u>
    Ⓒ hilly <u>terrain</u>
    Ⓓ ocean <u>landscape</u>

20. Ⓐ <u>protective</u> custody
    Ⓑ <u>violent</u> storm
    Ⓒ <u>investigait</u> the murder
    Ⓓ <u>survive</u> the battle

STOP

STOP

Test 3: Language Mechanics/Usage (Form B)

Directions For questions 1–10 darken the circle for the word or words that best complete each sentence.

Sample A

The stars look _____ tonight than last night.

Ⓐ bright
Ⓑ brightest
Ⓒ brighter
Ⓓ brightly

Time: 28 minutes

1. I have _____ how to ride a bike since I was five.
   Ⓐ known
   Ⓑ knew
   Ⓒ know
   Ⓓ knowed

2. Last week I _____ my backpack.
   Ⓐ lose
   Ⓑ loser
   Ⓒ lost
   Ⓓ will lose

3. Can you come over _____ than noon?
   Ⓐ early
   Ⓑ earlier
   Ⓒ earliest
   Ⓓ earlyed

4. This ice cream is the _____ I've ever eaten.
   Ⓐ smooth
   Ⓑ smoother
   Ⓒ smoothly
   Ⓓ smoothest

5. Last month we _____ at the beach.
   Ⓐ swim
   Ⓑ swam
   Ⓒ have swum
   Ⓓ swimming

6. An apple _____ a good snack.
   Ⓐ is
   Ⓑ are
   Ⓒ were
   Ⓓ aren't

7. _____ been to my school before.
   Ⓐ They're
   Ⓑ They'll
   Ⓒ They've
   Ⓓ They

8. Ricky is the _____ player on the team.
   Ⓐ more best
   Ⓑ good
   Ⓒ better
   Ⓓ best

9. Dad and _____ are going fishing.
   Ⓐ me
   Ⓑ I
   Ⓒ myself
   Ⓓ mine

10. Mom got a video for _____ to watch.
    Ⓐ me
    Ⓑ I
    Ⓒ mine
    Ⓓ myself

GO ON ⇨

Test 3: Language Mechanics/Usage (Form B), page 2

Directions For questions 11–20 darken the circle for the phrase in each sentence that shows the complete subject or the complete predicate.

Sample B
What is the complete predicate of this sentence?

The coach taught us how to shoot baskets.

Ⓐ taught
Ⓑ The coach
Ⓒ shoot baskets
Ⓓ taught us how to shoot baskets

11. **What is the complete subject of this sentence?**

Ray works at a vet clinic.

Ⓐ vet clinic
Ⓑ Ray works
Ⓒ works at a vet clinic
Ⓓ Ray

12. **What is the complete predicate of this sentence?**

The small plane bounced as we landed.

Ⓐ bounced as we landed
Ⓑ The small plane
Ⓒ bounced
Ⓓ as we landed

13. **What is the complete subject of this sentence?**

Our junior high school was built last year.

Ⓐ Our
Ⓑ Our junior high school
Ⓒ was built last year
Ⓓ school was built

14. **What is the complete predicate of this sentence?**

We didn't understand where to meet.

Ⓐ We
Ⓑ didn't understand where to meet
Ⓒ to meet
Ⓓ understand

15. **What is the complete subject of this sentence?**

None of my friends went to camp.

Ⓐ None
Ⓑ friends went
Ⓒ None of my friends
Ⓓ went to camp

16. **What is the complete predicate of this sentence?**

My aunt is baking a pie for me.

Ⓐ My aunt
Ⓑ is baking a pie for me
Ⓒ for me
Ⓓ is baking

17. **What is the complete subject of this sentence?**

Mom, Dad, and I watched my sister perform.

Ⓐ watched my sister perform
Ⓑ my sister
Ⓒ Mom, Dad, and I
Ⓓ I watched my sister

18. **What is the complete predicate of this sentence?**

Dan and Terri walked to the bus stop.

Ⓐ Dan and Terri
Ⓑ walked to the bus stop
Ⓒ to the bus
Ⓓ walked

GO ON ⇨

Test 3: Language Mechanics/Usage (Form B), page 3

19. What is the complete subject of this sentence?

A roomy minivan holds a lot of people.

Ⓐ A roomy minivan
Ⓑ a lot of people
Ⓒ holds a lot of people
Ⓓ minivan

20. What is the complete predicate of this sentence?

My brother raked and bagged the leaves.

Ⓐ My brother
Ⓑ the leaves
Ⓒ raked and bagged the leaves
Ⓓ raked the leaves

Directions For questions 21–28 darken the circle for the sentence that shows correct capitalization and punctuation.

Sample C

Ⓐ Cape canaveral is in florida.
Ⓑ New Year's Day is January 1.
Ⓒ What is your middle name.
Ⓓ My dentists office is downtown.

21. Ⓐ We drove to see lake ontario.
Ⓑ The Rock and Roll Hall of Fame is in Cleveland.
Ⓒ Tim and i played video games on Saturday.
Ⓓ Let's order french toast and cocoa.

22. Ⓐ Dr. Willie Brown is Superintendent of Schools.
Ⓑ Radio City music hall is in New York.
Ⓒ Were you at the birthday party.
Ⓓ "Dick when will you be over?" asked Jill.

23. Ⓐ One boys' bike was missing.
Ⓑ Take off your hat inside the house please.
Ⓒ Don't touch that poisonous spider!
Ⓓ Sammi asked where is my mom?

24. Ⓐ I like salt pepper and mustard on hot dogs.
Ⓑ On Friday, April 5, we'll have a concert.
Ⓒ Let me introduce you to Tony?
Ⓓ Lucys report was about fossils.

25. Ⓐ Have you ever traveled by light rail.
Ⓑ The Amon Carter museum of art is in Ft. Worth.
Ⓒ "Boy Breaking Glass" is a poem by Gwendolyn Brooks.
Ⓓ Mr. and mrs. Valiant live next door.

26. Ⓐ What time will the circus parade begin!
Ⓑ The american people love to eat pizza.
Ⓒ He bought one quarter's worth of candy.
Ⓓ Mayor thomas won a close election.

GO ON ⇨

Test 3: Language Mechanics/Usage
(Form B), page 4

27. Ⓐ March April and May are spring months.
    Ⓑ Who won the nobel peace prize this year?
    Ⓒ Food from the cats' dishes spilled on the floor.
    Ⓓ Soccer is the worlds most popular sport.

28. Ⓐ Labor day is the first monday in September.
    Ⓑ "Oh I didn't mean to step on you," he said.
    Ⓒ Turn left, then turn right on hart lane.
    Ⓓ Mrs. Johnson is a grandmother.

Directions For questions 29–34 darken the circle for the choice that shows the correct capitalization and punctuation for the underlined part of each sentence. Darken the circle for *Correct as it is* if there is no error.

Sample D

The <u>Halls house</u> has holiday decorations.
Ⓐ Halls'es house
Ⓑ Halls' house
Ⓒ Hall's house'
Ⓓ Correct as it is

29. After the play is <u>over we'll</u> go out to dinner.
    Ⓐ over, we'll
    Ⓑ over; we'll
    Ⓒ over we'll
    Ⓓ Correct as it is

30. I need to buy wrapping <u>paper ribbons and</u> bows.
    Ⓐ paper ribbons, and
    Ⓑ , paper, ribbons, and,
    Ⓒ paper, ribbons, and
    Ⓓ Correct as it is

31. Do you know where to buy the <u>tickets?</u>
    Ⓐ tickets!
    Ⓑ tickets.
    Ⓒ tickets,
    Ⓓ Correct as it is

32. Martin Luther King, Jr., was born on <u>January 15 1929</u>.
    Ⓐ January 15, 1929
    Ⓑ January, 15, 1929
    Ⓒ , January, 15 1929
    Ⓓ Correct as it is

33. Mrs. <u>Kyle the librarian helped</u> us find books.
    Ⓐ Kyle: the librarian helped
    Ⓑ Kyle "the librarian" helped
    Ⓒ Kyle, the librarian, helped
    Ⓓ Correct as it is

34. The <u>womens shoes</u> are on sale today.
    Ⓐ womens' shoes
    Ⓑ women's shoes
    Ⓒ womens shoes'
    Ⓓ Correct as it is

STOP

STOP

Test 4: Language Expression (Form B)

Directions For questions 1–6 darken the circle for the sentence that best combines the underlined sentences.

Sample A

The truck dumped a load of gravel. The gravel was dumped onto the driveway.

Ⓐ Onto the driveway was a load of gravel dumped by the truck.

Ⓑ A load of gravel was dumped by a truck onto the driveway.

Ⓒ The truck dumped a load of gravel onto the driveway.

Ⓓ Dumped onto the driveway was a load of gravel that was dumped by a truck.

Time: 15 minutes

1. My brother gave a speech. He was at school.

Ⓐ At school a speech was given by my brother.

Ⓑ A speech by my brother was given at school.

Ⓒ My brother he went to school and gave a speech.

Ⓓ My brother gave a speech at school.

2. Dad put our car up for sale. The car was used.

Ⓐ Dad put our used car up for sale.

Ⓑ Up for sale our used car was put by Dad.

Ⓒ Dad put our car up for sale it was used.

Ⓓ The used car was put up for sale by Dad.

3. We wanted to visit our grandparents. We went on a trip.

Ⓐ To visit our grandparents we wanted to do and on a trip we went.

Ⓑ We wanted to visit our grandparents without we went on a trip.

Ⓒ We wanted to visit our grandparents, so we went on a trip.

Ⓓ On a trip we went so our grandparents we wanted to visit.

4. We made two cakes for the birthday. The cakes are made of chocolate.

Ⓐ For the birthday two chocolate cakes were made by us.

Ⓑ Two cakes are made of chocolate and made for the birthday.

Ⓒ Made of chocolate are two cakes we made for the birthday.

Ⓓ We made two chocolate cakes for the birthday.

5. Where is the dog? I asked you to put him outside.

Ⓐ Where is the dog that I asked you to put outside?

Ⓑ The dog that I asked you to put outside, where is he?

Ⓒ Where is he, the dog that I asked you to put outside?

Ⓓ Where is the dog I asked you to put him outside.

GO ON ⇨

Test 4: Language Expression
(Form B), page 2

6. <u>Randy's shirt got torn.</u>
<u>The shirt was caught on a tree branch.</u>

Ⓐ Randy's shirt it got torn caught on a tree branch.

Ⓑ When it got caught on a tree branch, so Randy's shirt got torn.

Ⓒ Randy's shirt got torn when it was caught on a tree branch.

Ⓓ Whenever Randy's shirt got torn, then it caught on a tree branch.

> **Directions** For questions 7–12 read the selection. Then darken the circle for the correct answer to each question.

If you like thrills, excitement, and speed, try snowboarding. [1] It is a combination of surfing, skateboarding, and skiing. [2] You can zoom down mountain slopes doing wheelies spins and hops. [3] A snowboard looks like a ski but is much wider. [4] Both feet are held onto it with bindings. [5] You stand on the board sideways, facing the direction you want to go. [6] Then you bend your knees and begin to glide down the hill use your toes and heels against the edges of the board to change direction and to stop. [7] Your size and weight are important to consider when buying one. [8] The first two days are rough because you'll fall a lot. [9] But after you get the hang of it, you'll have great fun and get exercise, too! [10]

7. Which is the topic sentence?

Ⓐ Sentence 5

Ⓑ Sentence 1

Ⓒ Sentence 4

Ⓓ Sentence 8

8. Which sentence doesn't belong in the paragraph?

Ⓐ Sentence 5

Ⓑ Sentence 2

Ⓒ Sentence 10

Ⓓ Sentence 8

9. Which is a run-on sentence?

Ⓐ Sentence 7

Ⓑ Sentence 9

Ⓒ Sentence 6

Ⓓ Sentence 3

10. Which sentences could be combined?

Ⓐ Sentences 3 and 4

Ⓑ Sentences 4 and 5

Ⓒ Sentences 8 and 9

Ⓓ Sentences 7 and 8

11. Which sentence has incorrect punctuation?

Ⓐ Sentence 1

Ⓑ Sentence 2

Ⓒ Sentence 3

Ⓓ Sentence 4

12. Which sentences have contractions?

Ⓐ Sentences 2 and 3

Ⓑ Sentences 4 and 6

Ⓒ Sentences 3 and 5

Ⓓ Sentences 9 and 10

STOP

STOP

Test 5: Mathematics Computation (Form A)

Directions For questions 1–40 darken the circle for the correct answer. Darken the circle for *Not given* if the correct answer is *not* given. Always reduce fractions to lowest terms.

Sample A

$65 + 782 =$

Ⓐ 974
Ⓑ 847
Ⓒ 747
Ⓓ Not given

Sample B

$680 - 213 =$

Ⓐ 3,677
Ⓑ 367
Ⓒ 467
Ⓓ Not given

Sample C

$87 \times 47 =$

Ⓐ 4,089
Ⓑ 4,890
Ⓒ 5,089
Ⓓ Not given

Sample D

$195 \div 3 =$

Ⓐ 63
Ⓑ 85
Ⓒ 56
Ⓓ Not given

Time: 25 minutes

1. $91 + 37 =$
   Ⓐ 138
   Ⓑ 128
   Ⓒ 1217
   Ⓓ Not given

2.   55
   $+ 75$

   Ⓐ 125
   Ⓑ 135
   Ⓒ 120
   Ⓓ Not given

3. $\frac{5}{8} + \frac{1}{8} =$
   Ⓐ $\frac{6}{16}$
   Ⓑ $\frac{3}{4}$
   Ⓒ $\frac{3}{8}$
   Ⓓ Not given

4.   3.29
   $+ 2.25$

   Ⓐ 5.54
   Ⓑ 6.44
   Ⓒ 5.44
   Ⓓ Not given

5.   392
       741
   $+ 747$

   Ⓐ 1,980
   Ⓑ 1,981
   Ⓒ 1,880
   Ⓓ Not given

GO ON ⇨

Test 5: Mathematics Computation
(Form A), page 2

6. 149 + 753 + 531 =
- Ⓐ 1,562
- Ⓑ 1,343
- Ⓒ 1,234
- Ⓓ Not given

7. $\frac{3}{6} + \frac{2}{6} =$
- Ⓐ $\frac{5}{12}$
- Ⓑ $\frac{5}{6}$
- Ⓒ $\frac{1}{2}$
- Ⓓ Not given

8. 772 + 125 =
- Ⓐ 997
- Ⓑ 897
- Ⓒ 887
- Ⓓ Not given

9. 985
    453
  + 238

- Ⓐ 1,576
- Ⓑ 1,876
- Ⓒ 1,676
- Ⓓ Not given

10. 4,075 + 279 + 3,457 =
- Ⓐ 7,801
- Ⓑ 7,811
- Ⓒ 7,001
- Ⓓ Not given

11. 836
     – 449

- Ⓐ 487
- Ⓑ 497
- Ⓒ 493
- Ⓓ Not given

12. 855 – 436 =
- Ⓐ 411
- Ⓑ 519
- Ⓒ 419
- Ⓓ Not given

13. 318 – 66 =
- Ⓐ 252
- Ⓑ 352
- Ⓒ 242
- Ⓓ Not given

14. $ 7.80
     – 3.41

- Ⓐ $5.49
- Ⓑ $4.59
- Ⓒ $4.39
- Ⓓ Not given

15. 613 – 422 =
- Ⓐ 192
- Ⓑ 291
- Ⓒ 181
- Ⓓ Not given

GO ON ⇨

Test 5: Mathematics Computation
(Form A), page 3

16. $\frac{7}{8} - \frac{3}{8} =$

Ⓐ $\frac{1}{2}$

Ⓑ $\frac{4}{16}$

Ⓒ $\frac{5}{8}$

Ⓓ Not given

17. $8\frac{5}{9}$
      $-4\frac{2}{9}$

Ⓐ $\frac{3}{9}$

Ⓑ $4\frac{1}{3}$

Ⓒ $\frac{4}{23}$

Ⓓ Not given

18. $2,460.12
     $-1,724.48$

Ⓐ $735.64

Ⓑ $1,735.64

Ⓒ $835.60

Ⓓ Not given

19. $6,000 - 2,630 =$

Ⓐ 4,460

Ⓑ 3,470

Ⓒ 3,380

Ⓓ Not given

20. $6,208 - 4,107 =$

Ⓐ 2,202

Ⓑ 2,201

Ⓒ 2,101

Ⓓ Not given

21. $6 \times 43 =$

Ⓐ 49

Ⓑ 258

Ⓒ 109

Ⓓ Not given

22. 86
      $\times\ 7$

Ⓐ 602

Ⓑ 642

Ⓒ 564

Ⓓ Not given

23. 3.000
      $\times\ 462$

Ⓐ 1,387.386

Ⓑ 1,386.286

Ⓒ 13,873.86

Ⓓ Not given

24. $69.5 \times 0.47 =$

Ⓐ 326.65

Ⓑ 3.2665

Ⓒ 32.665

Ⓓ Not given

25. $4.3 \times 86 =$

Ⓐ 3,698

Ⓑ 3.698

Ⓒ 36.98

Ⓓ Not given

GO ON ⇨

Test 5: Mathematics Computation
(Form A), page 4

26. $ 315.50
    $\times$ 8

  Ⓐ $ 2,423.00
  Ⓑ $ 2,524.80
  Ⓒ $ 2,524.00
  Ⓓ Not given

27. $\frac{1}{2} \times \frac{5}{10} =$
  Ⓐ $\frac{1}{8}$
  Ⓑ $\frac{6}{20}$
  Ⓒ $\frac{6}{10}$
  Ⓓ Not given

28. $735 \times \frac{6}{7} =$
  Ⓐ 4,410
  Ⓑ   630
  Ⓒ   560
  Ⓓ Not given

29. $7\frac{1}{2} \times$ ___ $= 6\frac{1}{4}$
  Ⓐ $\frac{1}{2}$
  Ⓑ $\frac{2}{3}$
  Ⓒ $\frac{5}{6}$
  Ⓓ Not given

30.   741
    $\times$ 25

  Ⓐ 14,820
  Ⓑ 18,525
  Ⓒ   3,705
  Ⓓ Not given

31. $5\overline{)748}$
  Ⓐ 149
  Ⓑ 150
  Ⓒ 149 R3
  Ⓓ Not given

32. $38 \div 12 =$
  Ⓐ 3 R2
  Ⓑ 6
  Ⓒ 4 R1
  Ⓓ Not given

33. $\frac{4}{5} \div \frac{1}{3} =$
  Ⓐ $\frac{3}{5}$
  Ⓑ $\frac{4}{15}$
  Ⓒ $1\frac{2}{5}$
  Ⓓ Not given

34. $2 \div \frac{2}{5} =$
  Ⓐ 2
  Ⓑ $1\frac{1}{5}$
  Ⓒ $1\frac{2}{5}$
  Ⓓ Not given

35. $9\overline{)64.17}$
  Ⓐ 0.713
  Ⓑ 7.13
  Ⓒ 71.3
  Ⓓ Not given

GO ON ⇨

Test 5: Mathematics Computation
(Form A), page 5

36. $30\overline{)7,143}$

Ⓐ 238
Ⓑ 240
Ⓒ 238 R3
Ⓓ Not given

37. $2,508 \div 8 =$

Ⓐ 313 R4
Ⓑ 314 R2
Ⓒ 316
Ⓓ Not given

38. $2,736 \div 8 =$

Ⓐ 34 R2
Ⓑ 342
Ⓒ 344
Ⓓ Not given

39. $18\overline{)8.28}$

Ⓐ 0.46
Ⓑ 4.6
Ⓒ 46
Ⓓ Not given

40. $\frac{3}{10} \div \frac{1}{2} =$

Ⓐ $\frac{4}{20}$
Ⓑ $\frac{1}{5}$
Ⓒ $\frac{3}{5}$
Ⓓ Not given

STOP

STOP

Test 5: Mathematics Computation (Form B)

Directions For questions 1–40 darken the circle for the correct answer. Darken the circle for *Not given* if the correct answer is *not* given. Always reduce fractions to lowest terms.

Sample A

47 + 873 =

Ⓐ 830
Ⓑ 820
Ⓒ 920
Ⓓ Not given

Sample B

564 − 213 =

Ⓐ 347
Ⓑ 351
Ⓒ 251
Ⓓ Not given

Sample C

49 × 38 =

Ⓐ 862
Ⓑ 1,962
Ⓒ 1,852
Ⓓ Not given

Sample D

196 ÷ 5 =

Ⓐ 39 R1
Ⓑ 49
Ⓒ 41 R1
Ⓓ Not given

Time: 25 minutes

1. 91 + 37 =
   Ⓐ 128
   Ⓑ 138
   Ⓒ 228
   Ⓓ Not given

2.   5,396
     + 4,817

   Ⓐ 9,203
   Ⓑ 10,313
   Ⓒ 10,213
   Ⓓ Not given

3. $\frac{1}{8} + \frac{3}{8} =$
   Ⓐ $\frac{1}{2}$
   Ⓑ $\frac{4}{16}$
   Ⓒ $\frac{1}{4}$
   Ⓓ Not given

4. $\frac{1}{6} + \frac{1}{2} =$
   Ⓐ $\frac{2}{6}$
   Ⓑ $\frac{2}{3}$
   Ⓒ $\frac{2}{8}$
   Ⓓ Not given

5.   38
       22
     + 57

   Ⓐ 107
   Ⓑ 127
   Ⓒ 117
   Ⓓ Not given

GO ON ⇨

Test 5: Mathematics Computation (Form B), page 2

6.   341
     109
     228
  + 164

   Ⓐ 842
   Ⓑ 942
   Ⓒ 852
   Ⓓ Not given

7. $938 + 79 + 421 =$
   Ⓐ 1,540
   Ⓑ 2,439
   Ⓒ 1,438
   Ⓓ Not given

8. $\frac{9}{24} + \frac{3}{24} =$
   Ⓐ $\frac{1}{2}$
   Ⓑ $\frac{12}{48}$
   Ⓒ $\frac{1}{4}$
   Ⓓ Not given

9.   5,702
  + 4,817

   Ⓐ 10,509
   Ⓑ 10,619
   Ⓒ 10,519
   Ⓓ Not given

10. $\frac{2}{3} + \frac{1}{4} =$
   Ⓐ $\frac{3}{7}$
   Ⓑ $\frac{11}{12}$
   Ⓒ $\frac{3}{4}$
   Ⓓ Not given

11.   721
  − 358

   Ⓐ 463
   Ⓑ 363
   Ⓒ 367
   Ⓓ Not given

12. $53.61
  − 28.05

   Ⓐ $25.56
   Ⓑ $24.56
   Ⓒ $25.06
   Ⓓ Not given

13. $9,371 − 4,528 =$
   Ⓐ 4,843
   Ⓑ 3,933
   Ⓒ 4,853
   Ⓓ Not given

14. $\frac{7}{10} - \frac{5}{10} =$
   Ⓐ $\frac{3}{10}$
   Ⓑ $\frac{1}{5}$
   Ⓒ $\frac{2}{5}$
   Ⓓ Not given

15. $\frac{3}{8} - \frac{1}{3} =$
   Ⓐ $\frac{1}{6}$
   Ⓑ $\frac{1}{24}$
   Ⓒ $\frac{2}{5}$
   Ⓓ Not given

GO ON ⇨

Test 5: Mathematics Computation
(Form B), page 3

16. $\frac{2}{3} - \frac{1}{2} =$
- Ⓐ $\frac{1}{6}$
- Ⓑ $\frac{1}{2}$
- Ⓒ $\frac{1}{3}$
- Ⓓ Not given

17. 6.134
  $- 2.583$

- Ⓐ 35.51
- Ⓑ 3.551
- Ⓒ 355.1
- Ⓓ Not given

18. $9\frac{1}{4}$
  $-2\frac{1}{2}$

- Ⓐ $8\frac{5}{4}$
- Ⓑ $2\frac{1}{2}$
- Ⓒ $6\frac{3}{4}$
- Ⓓ Not given

19. $2\frac{3}{4} - 1\frac{1}{2} =$
- Ⓐ $1\frac{1}{2}$
- Ⓑ $1\frac{1}{4}$
- Ⓒ $2\frac{1}{4}$
- Ⓓ Not given

20. 6,000
  $- 3,781$

- Ⓐ 2,219
- Ⓑ 2,319
- Ⓒ 2,329
- Ⓓ Not given

21. $45 \times 100 =$
- Ⓐ 4,000
- Ⓑ 1,500
- Ⓒ 4,500
- Ⓓ Not given

22. 328
  $\times\ 43$

- Ⓐ 13,120
- Ⓑ 14,004
- Ⓒ 13,401
- Ⓓ Not given

23. $1.9 \times 0.8 =$
- Ⓐ 152
- Ⓑ 1.52
- Ⓒ 15.2
- Ⓓ Not given

24. 5.27
  $\times\ 7.8$

- Ⓐ 41.106
- Ⓑ 42.106
- Ⓒ 41.116
- Ⓓ Not given

25. $\frac{5}{2} \times \frac{4}{3} =$
- Ⓐ $\frac{6}{9}$
- Ⓑ $3\frac{1}{3}$
- Ⓒ $2\frac{2}{3}$
- Ⓓ Not given

GO ON ⇨

Test 5: Mathematics Computation
(Form B), page 4

26. $9\frac{1}{3} \times \frac{2}{6} =$

  Ⓐ $2\frac{2}{9}$

  Ⓑ $3\frac{2}{9}$

  Ⓒ $3\frac{1}{8}$

  Ⓓ Not given

27. $\frac{2}{5} \times$ ___ $= 10$

  Ⓐ 50

  Ⓑ 25

  Ⓒ 35

  Ⓓ Not given

28.   56
    $\times 25$

  Ⓐ 1,120

  Ⓑ 1,320

  Ⓒ 1,400

  Ⓓ Not given

29. $73.18
    $\times\ 6.00$

  Ⓐ $439.08

  Ⓑ $430.80

  Ⓒ $420.80

  Ⓓ Not given

30.   224
    $\times 105$

  Ⓐ 23,520

  Ⓑ 23,502

  Ⓒ 23,052

  Ⓓ Not given

31. $2,992 \div 8 =$

  Ⓐ 351

  Ⓑ 374

  Ⓒ 382

  Ⓓ Not given

32. $48\overline{)1,594}$

  Ⓐ 33 R10

  Ⓑ 34 R9

  Ⓒ 33 R8

  Ⓓ Not given

33. $\frac{7}{3} \div \frac{?}{6} = 2\frac{4}{5}$

  Ⓐ 3

  Ⓑ 4

  Ⓒ 5

  Ⓓ Not given

34. $\frac{7}{12} \div \frac{1}{6} =$

  Ⓐ $3\frac{1}{2}$

  Ⓑ $2\frac{3}{4}$

  Ⓒ $3\frac{1}{4}$

  Ⓓ Not given

35. $9\overline{)34.29}$

  Ⓐ 38.1

  Ⓑ 3.81

  Ⓒ .381

  Ⓓ Not given

GO ON ⇨

Test 5: Mathematics Computation
(Form B), page 5

36. 156 ÷ 20 =
  (A) 8
  (B) 7 R12
  (C) 7 R16
  (D) Not given

37. 336 ÷ 42 =
  (A) 8
  (B) 7 R6
  (C) 9
  (D) Not given

38. $33\overline{)298}$

  (A) 9
  (B) 9 R1
  (C) 9 R3
  (D) Not given

39. 6.517 ÷ 7 =
  (A) .931
  (B) 93.1
  (C) 9.31
  (D) Not given

40. $28\overline{)7}$

  (A) 2.50
  (B) 0.25
  (C) 25
  (D) Not given

STOP

Test 6: Mathematics Concepts/Applications: Numeration/Number Theory (Form A)

Directions For questions 1–18 darken the circle for the correct answer. Darken the circle for *Not given* if the correct answer is *not* given.

Sample A

Which is the correct way to write the standard form for these number words?

forty-six thousand, three hundred eight

Ⓐ 4,6308
Ⓑ 46,380
Ⓒ 46,308
Ⓓ Not given

Sample B

Which are factors of 56?

Ⓐ 7, 8
Ⓑ 11, 5
Ⓒ 8, 8
Ⓓ Not given

Time: 12 minutes

1. Round 25,831 to the nearest ten.
   Ⓐ 25,800
   Ⓑ 25,000
   Ⓒ 25,830
   Ⓓ Not given

2. In which place is the underlined digit?
   88,<u>8</u>88
   Ⓐ tens place
   Ⓑ hundreds place
   Ⓒ thousands place
   Ⓓ Not given

3. Which number has a 7 in the ten thousands place?
   Ⓐ 72,439
   Ⓑ 67,838
   Ⓒ 86,725
   Ⓓ Not given

4. Which is a true sentence?
   Ⓐ 629,387 > 89,974
   Ⓑ 427,600 < 426,700
   Ⓒ 99,999 > 100,000
   Ⓓ Not given

5. Round 451 to the nearest hundred.
   Ⓐ 400
   Ⓑ 450
   Ⓒ 500
   Ⓓ Not given

6. Which represents
   12,000 + 300 + 20 + 6?
   Ⓐ 12,326
   Ⓑ 12,306
   Ⓒ 12,263
   Ⓓ Not given

7. Which of these sets of numbers is ordered from the least to the greatest?
   Ⓐ 6208 3155 2542
   Ⓑ 3155 6208 2542
   Ⓒ 2542 3155 6208
   Ⓓ Not given

GO ON ⇨

Test 6: Mathematics Concepts/Applications: Numeration/Number Theory (Form A), page 2

8. Which is the standard number for CCCLXV?
   - Ⓐ 355
   - Ⓑ 265
   - Ⓒ 345
   - Ⓓ Not given

9. Which is the Roman numeral for 76?
   - Ⓐ LXXVI
   - Ⓑ XLXVI
   - Ⓒ XXLVI
   - Ⓓ Not given

10. Which is the expanded form of 2,493?
    - Ⓐ 2,000 + 49 + 3
    - Ⓑ 200 + 4 + 9 + 3
    - Ⓒ 2,000 + 400 + 90 + 3
    - Ⓓ Not given

11. Which of these is an odd number?
    - Ⓐ 317
    - Ⓑ 636
    - Ⓒ 456
    - Ⓓ Not given

12. What does the 7 in 6,871 mean?
    - Ⓐ seven hundred
    - Ⓑ seventy
    - Ⓒ seven
    - Ⓓ Not given

13. Which number is *not* evenly divisible by 3?
    - Ⓐ 99
    - Ⓑ 95
    - Ⓒ 93
    - Ⓓ Not given

14. Which fraction has the same value as 2.1?
    - Ⓐ $2\frac{1}{10}$
    - Ⓑ $2\frac{1}{2}$
    - Ⓒ $2\frac{1}{100}$
    - Ⓓ Not given

15. Which of these should you use to estimate 6,161 + 8,985?
    - Ⓐ 6,000 + 8,000
    - Ⓑ 6,000 + 9,000
    - Ⓒ 600 + 8,000
    - Ⓓ Not given

16. Which is the missing factor?
    $8 \times \underline{\quad} = 24$
    - Ⓐ 4
    - Ⓑ 2
    - Ⓒ 5
    - Ⓓ Not given

17. Which of these is equal to 8?
    - Ⓐ 8×0
    - Ⓑ 8×1
    - Ⓒ $0 \div 8$
    - Ⓓ Not given

18. What number is missing from this pattern?
    39, 35, ___, 27, 23
    - Ⓐ 29
    - Ⓑ 33
    - Ⓒ 31
    - Ⓓ Not given

STOP

STOP

Test 7: Mathematics Concepts/Applications: Geometry/Measurement (Form A)

Directions For questions 1–12 darken the circle for the correct answer. Darken the circle for *Not given* if the correct answer is *not* given.

Sample A

Which clock shows that the time is 6:45?

A　　　　　**B**　　　　　**C**

Ⓐ A
Ⓑ B
Ⓒ C
Ⓓ Not given

Sample B

Which of these figures shows a line of symmetry?

A　　**B**　　**C**　　**D**

Ⓐ A
Ⓑ B
Ⓒ C
Ⓓ Not given

Time: 10 minutes

1. Which numbers are on triangles in this figure?
   Ⓐ 3, 4, 2
   Ⓑ 2, 1, 5
   Ⓒ 4, 1, 3
   Ⓓ Not given

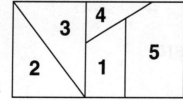

2. Which of these would fit into the rectangular figure shown above the groups of figures?

A　　　　　**B**　　　　　**C**

Ⓐ A
Ⓑ B
Ⓒ C
Ⓓ Not given

3. Which is the temperature shown on this thermometer?
   Ⓐ 10°
   Ⓑ −10°
   Ⓒ −5°
   Ⓓ Not given

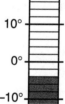

10°

0°

−10°

4. Which of these is a cylinder?
   Ⓐ D
   Ⓑ C
   Ⓒ A
   Ⓓ Not given

A　　　　　**B**

C　　　　　**D**

GO ON ⇨

Test 7: Mathematics Concepts/Applications: Geometry/Measurement (Form A), page 2

5. What portion of this circle is shaded?

ⓐ $\frac{1}{3}$
ⓑ $\frac{2}{3}$
ⓒ $\frac{1}{2}$
ⓓ Not given

6. What is the name of this figure?

ⓐ rectangle
ⓑ trapezoid
ⓒ parallelogram
ⓓ Not given

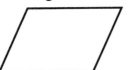

7. What time is $\frac{3}{4}$ of an hour after 12:15 P.M.?

ⓐ 1:00 P.M.
ⓑ 12:45 P.M.
ⓒ 11:45 P.M.
ⓓ Not given

8. What size paint container would you buy to paint a room?

ⓐ quart
ⓑ gill
ⓒ gallon
ⓓ Not given

9. How many triangles are in this figure?

ⓐ 6
ⓑ 8
ⓒ 5
ⓓ Not given

10. What is the perimeter of this figure?

ⓐ 36 inches
ⓑ 24 inches
ⓒ 18 inches
ⓓ Not given

11. What is the area of this rectangle?

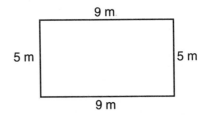

ⓐ 28 square meters
ⓑ 18 square meters
ⓒ 45 square meters
ⓓ Not given

12. Which is the name for these lines?

ⓐ intersecting
ⓑ perpendicular
ⓒ parallel
ⓓ Not given

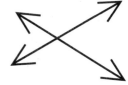

STOP

Test 8: Mathematics Concepts/Applications: Number Sentences/Ratios and Percents (Form A)

Directions For questions 1–20 darken the circle for the correct answer.

Sample A

What number completes this number sentence?

$4 + 4 + ? = 16$

Ⓐ 4
Ⓑ 7
Ⓒ 8
Ⓓ 9

Sample B

Which fraction shows the ratio of 17 to 15?

Ⓐ $\frac{17}{15}$
Ⓑ $\frac{15}{17}$
Ⓒ $1\frac{2}{15}$
Ⓓ $\frac{17}{25}$

Time: 15 minutes

1. Which pair of ratios is equal?
   Ⓐ $\frac{27}{54}, \frac{9}{18}$
   Ⓑ $\frac{12}{5}, \frac{4}{25}$
   Ⓒ $\frac{6}{12}, \frac{1}{12}$
   Ⓓ $\frac{7}{4}, \frac{35}{8}$

2. Which percent is the same as the ratio 89:100?
   Ⓐ 90%
   Ⓑ 89%
   Ⓒ 100%
   Ⓓ 11%

3. Change 2% to a decimal.
   Ⓐ 0.02
   Ⓑ 2.0
   Ⓒ 0.2
   Ⓓ 20.00

4. Change $\frac{9}{25}$ to a percent.
   Ⓐ 25%
   Ⓑ 90%
   Ⓒ 36%
   Ⓓ 10%

5. Which of these is correct?
   Ⓐ $9 \times 1 = 9$
   Ⓑ $9 \times 0 = 9$
   Ⓒ $9 \times 0 = 90$
   Ⓓ $9 \times 1 = 10$

6. Choose the correct operation.
   $2 \times 12 = 6 \;\square\; 4$
   Ⓐ +
   Ⓑ −
   Ⓒ ×
   Ⓓ ÷

7. Choose the correct operation.
   $81 \;\square\; 9 = 3 \times 3$
   Ⓐ +
   Ⓑ −
   Ⓒ ×
   Ⓓ ÷

8. Which number sentence shows correct placement of the < or > sign?
   Ⓐ $379 > 528$
   Ⓑ $723 < 841$
   Ⓒ $8 < 5$
   Ⓓ $25 > 27$

9. Complete this number sentence.
   $(2 + 5) + 9 = \underline{\quad} - 9$
   Ⓐ 17
   Ⓑ 16
   Ⓒ 25
   Ⓓ 27

GO ON ⇨

Test 8: Mathematics Concepts/Applications: Number Sentences/Ratios and Percents (Form A), page 2

10. If sales tax is 5%, what is the amount of tax on items that cost $1.78 and $2.36?

(A) 32¢

(B) 21¢

(C) 25¢

(D) 18¢

11. Find 16% of 42 using a decimal.

(A) 6.72

(B) 67.2

(C) 67.02

(D) 670.2

12. Find 10% of 120.

(A) 25

(B) 12

(C) 18

(D) 20

13. Use 10% to estimate 13% of 150.

(A) 13

(B) 18

(C) 10

(D) 15

Answer questions 14–17 based on a cube that has faces numbered 1–6.

14. What is the probability of the cube landing on an even number?

(A) 1:2

(B) 2:1

(C) 6:2

(D) 2:6

15. What is the probability of the cube landing on an odd number?

(A) 3:5

(B) 5:6

(C) 1:2

(D) 2:3

16. What is the probability of the cube landing on a prime number?

(A) 0

(B) 2:3

(C) 1:2

(D) 1:3

17. What is the probability of the cube landing on a number less than 4?

(A) $\frac{1}{3}$

(B) $\frac{1}{2}$

(C) $\frac{1}{6}$

(D) $\frac{3}{6}$

Answer questions 18–20 about these cards.

18. What is the probability of choosing a card with the letter *A*?

(A) $\frac{8}{10}$

(B) $\frac{1}{5}$

(C) $\frac{2}{5}$

(D) $\frac{4}{5}$

D   B   A   C   A

B   D   B   D   D

19. What is the probability of choosing a card with the letter *C*?

(A) $\frac{9}{10}$

(B) $\frac{7}{10}$

(C) $\frac{3}{10}$

(D) $\frac{1}{10}$

20. What is the probability of choosing a card with the letter *D*?

(A) $\frac{1}{2}$

(B) $\frac{2}{5}$

(C) $\frac{3}{5}$

(D) $\frac{2}{3}$

STOP

STOP

Test 9: Mathematics Concepts/Applications: Reading Charts and Graphs (Form A)

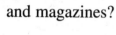**Directions** For questions 1–10 darken the circle for the correct answer.

Sample

What percent of his money does Miguel spend on lunch out and magazines?

Miguel's Earnings

- Ⓐ 45%
- Ⓑ 50%
- Ⓒ 5%
- Ⓓ 25%

Time: 15 minutes

1. How many students spent more than 1 hour a week reading?

   - Ⓐ 12 students
   - Ⓑ 18 students
   - Ⓒ 40 students
   - Ⓓ 34 students

Time Spent Reading Each Week

Hours	Number of Students
1	6
2	12
3	18
4	4

2. Which ordered pair represents point S on the grid?
   - Ⓐ 3, 3
   - Ⓑ 2, 3
   - Ⓒ 3, 2
   - Ⓓ 1, 3

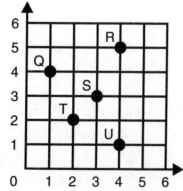

Use the graph to answer questions 3–5.

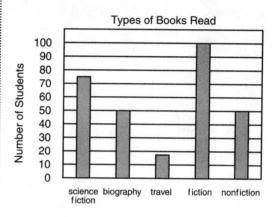

Types of Books Read

3. Which two categories of books were read by the same number of students?
   - Ⓐ science fiction and biography
   - Ⓑ travel and nonfiction
   - Ⓒ biography and nonfiction
   - Ⓓ fiction and science fiction

4. How many students read books on travel?
   - Ⓐ 10 students
   - Ⓑ 18 students
   - Ⓒ 20 students
   - Ⓓ 30 students

5. Which category of books was read by the most students?
   - Ⓐ fiction
   - Ⓑ science fiction
   - Ⓒ biography
   - Ⓓ nonfiction

GO ON ⇨

Test 9: Mathematics Concepts/Applications: Reading Charts and Graphs (Form A), page 2

Use the graph to answer questions 6–7.

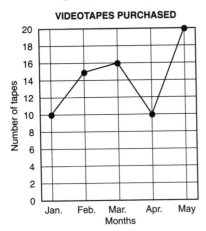

VIDEOTAPES PURCHASED

6. In what month did sales go down?
- Ⓐ February
- Ⓑ March
- Ⓒ April
- Ⓓ May

7. How many tapes were sold in February and March?
- Ⓐ 16 tapes
- Ⓑ 31 tapes
- Ⓒ 15 tapes
- Ⓓ 25 tapes

Use the graph to answer questions 8–10.

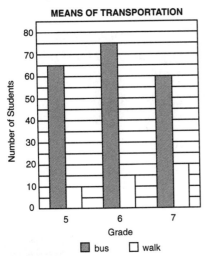

MEANS OF TRANSPORTATION

8. How many students in grade 6 walk to school?
- Ⓐ 15 students
- Ⓑ 10 students
- Ⓒ 75 students
- Ⓓ 20 students

9. How many students in all three grades walk to school?
- Ⓐ 35 students
- Ⓑ 60 students
- Ⓒ 45 students
- Ⓓ 30 students

10. In which grade do the fewest number of students take the bus?
- Ⓐ Grade 5
- Ⓑ Grade 6
- Ⓒ Grade 7
- Ⓓ Grades 5 and 6

STOP

Test 6: Mathematics Concepts/Applications: Numeration/Number Theory (Form B)

Directions For questions 1–18 darken the circle for the correct answer. Darken the circle for *Not given* if the correct answer is *not* given.

Sample A

Which is the correct standard number form for these number words?

fourteen thousand, thirty-nine

- Ⓐ 14,039
- Ⓑ 14,309
- Ⓒ 14,390
- Ⓓ Not given

Sample B

Which are factors of 63?

- Ⓐ 6, 3
- Ⓑ 4, 9
- Ⓒ 9, 7
- Ⓓ Not given

Time: 12 minutes

1. Round 52,017 to the nearest hundred.
   - Ⓐ 52,100
   - Ⓑ 52,000
   - Ⓒ 52,110
   - Ⓓ Not given

2. Which words mean the same as 536,402,360?
   - Ⓐ five hundred thirty-six million, forty-two thousand, three hundred six
   - Ⓑ five hundred thirty-six million, four hundred twenty thousand, three hundred sixty
   - Ⓒ five hundred thirty-six million, four hundred two thousand, three hundred sixty
   - Ⓓ Not given

3. What is the least common multiple of 3 and 4?
   - Ⓐ 9
   - Ⓑ 12
   - Ⓒ 6
   - Ⓓ Not given

4. Which of these has 3 in the ten thousands place?
   - Ⓐ 367,541
   - Ⓑ 36,497
   - Ⓒ 3,579
   - Ⓓ Not given

5. Which number is the least?
   - Ⓐ 200
   - Ⓑ 201
   - Ⓒ 199
   - Ⓓ 202

6. Which represents 68,000 + 900 + 70 + 2?
   - Ⓐ 68,900,072
   - Ⓑ 68,090,072
   - Ⓒ 68,972
   - Ⓓ Not given

7. Which of these sets of numbers is ordered from greatest to least?
   - Ⓐ 4,729   2,678   5,270
   - Ⓑ 5,270   2,678   4,729
   - Ⓒ 5,270   4,729   2,678
   - Ⓓ Not given

GO ON ⇨

Test 6: Mathematics Concepts/Applications: Numeration/Number Theory (Form B), page 2

8. Which is the standard number for MDCLXIII?
- Ⓐ 1,563
- Ⓑ 1,663
- Ⓒ 1,553
- Ⓓ Not given

9. Which is the Roman numeral for 128?
- Ⓐ CVIII
- Ⓑ CVXXIII
- Ⓒ CXXIIIV
- Ⓓ Not given

10. What does the 6 in 36,839 mean?
- Ⓐ six thousand
- Ⓑ sixty thousand
- Ⓒ six hundred
- Ⓓ Not given

11. Which is the expanded form of 5,013?
- Ⓐ 5,000 + 13
- Ⓑ 5,000 + 100 + 3
- Ⓒ 5,000 + 10 + 3
- Ⓓ Not given

12. Which of these is an even number?
- Ⓐ 38
- Ⓑ 29
- Ⓒ 75
- Ⓓ Not given

13. Which of these should you use to estimate 2,106 – 1,481?
- Ⓐ 2,200 – 1,500
- Ⓑ 2,000 – 1,300
- Ⓒ 2,100 – 1,500
- Ⓓ Not given

14. Which number is evenly divisible by 7?
- Ⓐ 63
- Ⓑ 59
- Ⓒ 87
- Ⓓ Not given

15. Which fraction has the same value as 1.5?
- Ⓐ $1\frac{1}{2}$
- Ⓑ $1\frac{5}{100}$
- Ⓒ $1\frac{1}{3}$
- Ⓓ Not given

16. Which is the standard numeral for nine and three hundred forty-two thousandths?
- Ⓐ 93.42
- Ⓑ 934.2
- Ⓒ 9.342
- Ⓓ Not given

17. Which number would be 40 if rounded to the nearest ten?
- Ⓐ 32
- Ⓑ 37
- Ⓒ 29
- Ⓓ Not given

18. Which number is missing in this pattern?
30, 24, 18, _____, 6
- Ⓐ 12
- Ⓑ 14
- Ⓒ 16
- Ⓓ Not given

STOP

STOP

Test 7: Mathematics Concepts/Applications: Geometry/Measurement (Form B)

Directions For questions 1–12 darken the circle for the correct answer. Darken the circle for *Not given* if the correct answer is *not* given.

Sample A

How many ounces of liquid can this cup hold?

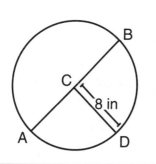

Ⓐ 4 ounces

Ⓑ 1 ounce

Ⓒ 8 ounces

Ⓓ Not given

Sample B

Which of these is a radius?

Ⓐ AB

Ⓑ CD

Ⓒ BD

Ⓓ Not given

Time: 10 minutes

1. Which of these is a chord?

Ⓐ AX

Ⓑ AB

Ⓒ BX

Ⓓ Not given

2. What is the perimeter of this figure?

Ⓐ 24 cm

Ⓑ 12 cm

Ⓒ 36 cm

Ⓓ Not given

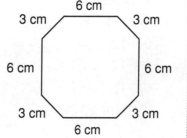

3. What fraction of this figure is shaded?

Ⓐ $\frac{3}{4}$

Ⓑ $\frac{3}{8}$

Ⓒ $\frac{6}{8}$

Ⓓ Not given

4. Which of these does not have a triangle congruent with the other shaded triangles?

   1   2   3   4

Ⓐ 2

Ⓑ 1

Ⓒ 4

Ⓓ Not given

5. What is the temperature on this thermometer?

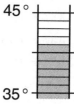

Ⓐ 45°

Ⓑ 39°

Ⓒ 41°

Ⓓ Not given

6. Which has a greater value than 82 cents?

Ⓐ 18 nickels

Ⓑ 3 quarters

Ⓒ 8 dimes

Ⓓ Not given

GO ON ⇨

Test 7: Mathematics Concepts/Applications: Geometry/Measurement (Form B), page 2

Use the calendar to answer questions 7–9.

November

Sun	Mon	Tues	Wed	Thur	Fri	Sat
			1	2	3	4
5	6	7	8	9	10	11
12	13	14	15	16	17	18
19	20	21	22	23	24	25
26	27	28	29	30		

7. The fourth Wednesday of this month falls on which date?
- Ⓐ 15
- Ⓑ 1
- Ⓒ 29
- Ⓓ Not given

8. On which day of the week does November 11 fall?
- Ⓐ Sunday
- Ⓑ Saturday
- Ⓒ Monday
- Ⓓ Not given

9. What is the date of the third Sunday of this month?
- Ⓐ 19
- Ⓑ 18
- Ⓒ 12
- Ⓓ Not given

10. What is the perimeter of this figure?
- Ⓐ 17 inches
- Ⓑ 15 inches
- Ⓒ 32 inches
- Ⓓ Not given

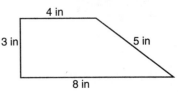

11. How are these figures alike?

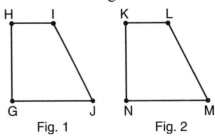

Fig. 1   Fig. 2

- Ⓐ They are perpendicular.
- Ⓑ They are congruent.
- Ⓒ They are intersecting.
- Ⓓ Not given

12. What is the name of this figure?
- Ⓐ trapezoid
- Ⓑ rhombus
- Ⓒ rectangle
- Ⓓ Not given

STOP

STOP

Name _____ Date _____

Test 8: Mathematics Concepts/Applications: Number Sentences/Ratios and Percents (Form B)

Directions For questions 1–20 darken the circle for the correct answer.

Sample A

What number completes this sentence?

$6 + 26 + ? = 45$

Ⓐ 20
Ⓑ 13
Ⓒ 15
Ⓓ 9

Sample B

Which fraction shows a ratio of 25 to 1?

Ⓐ $\frac{1}{25}$
Ⓑ $1\frac{2}{5}$
Ⓒ $\frac{25}{1}$
Ⓓ $2\frac{5}{1}$

Time: 15 minutes

1. What number makes this number sentence true?

$18 \times ? = 0$

Ⓐ 0
Ⓑ 1
Ⓒ 10
Ⓓ 18

2. Which pair of ratios is equal?

Ⓐ $\frac{3}{1}, \frac{12}{4}$
Ⓑ $\frac{3}{2}, \frac{6}{10}$
Ⓒ $\frac{3}{2}, \frac{7}{4}$
Ⓓ $\frac{9}{6}, \frac{12}{18}$

3. Which percent equals $\frac{17}{100}$?

Ⓐ 70%
Ⓑ 17%
Ⓒ 100%
Ⓓ 71%

4. Which is the decimal for 38%?

Ⓐ 0.38
Ⓑ 3.8
Ⓒ 3.08
Ⓓ 30.8

5. Which is the fraction for 20%?

Ⓐ $\frac{3}{5}$
Ⓑ $\frac{4}{5}$
Ⓒ $\frac{1}{5}$
Ⓓ $\frac{2}{5}$

6. A ratio is a way of _____ numbers.

Ⓐ adding
Ⓑ comparing
Ⓒ dividing
Ⓓ changing

7. Choose the correct operation.

$72 \;\square\; 9 = 15 - 7$

Ⓐ +
Ⓑ −
Ⓒ ×
Ⓓ ÷

8. Which number sentence is true?

Ⓐ 864 < 863
Ⓑ 792 > 690
Ⓒ 849 > 853
Ⓓ 60,000 < 59,999

9. Complete this number sentence.

$414 \times 5 = 1,035 \times ?$

Ⓐ 2
Ⓑ 6
Ⓒ 3
Ⓓ 4

GO ON ⇨

Test 8: Mathematics Concepts/Applications: Number Sentences/Ratios and Percents (Form B), page 2

10. Find 50% of 92.
 Ⓐ 50
 Ⓑ 46
 Ⓒ 54
 Ⓓ 44

11. Find 39% of 47 using a decimal.
 Ⓐ 1.833
 Ⓑ 18.33
 Ⓒ 183.3
 Ⓓ 1.083

12. If sales tax is 5%, what is the tax on $12.90?
 Ⓐ 65¢
 Ⓑ 32¢
 Ⓒ 48¢
 Ⓓ 82¢

13. Use 25% to estimate 27% of 88.
 Ⓐ 45
 Ⓑ 36
 Ⓒ 22
 Ⓓ 25

14. Use 50% to estimate 53% of 244.
 Ⓐ 122
 Ⓑ 53
 Ⓒ 104
 Ⓓ 200

Answer questions 15–18 using these cards.

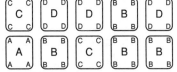

15. What is the probability of choosing a card with the letter *A*?
 Ⓐ $\frac{9}{10}$
 Ⓑ $\frac{1}{5}$
 Ⓒ $\frac{1}{10}$
 Ⓓ $\frac{2}{5}$

16. What is the probability of choosing a card with the letter *B*?
 Ⓐ $\frac{2}{5}$
 Ⓑ $\frac{6}{10}$
 Ⓒ $\frac{1}{10}$
 Ⓓ $\frac{4}{5}$

17. What is the probability of choosing a card with the letter *C*?
 Ⓐ $\frac{3}{5}$
 Ⓑ $\frac{3}{10}$
 Ⓒ $\frac{1}{5}$
 Ⓓ $\frac{2}{5}$

18. What is the probability of choosing a card with the letter *D*?
 Ⓐ $\frac{3}{10}$
 Ⓑ $\frac{1}{2}$
 Ⓒ $\frac{3}{5}$
 Ⓓ $\frac{7}{10}$

19. What percent of this circle is shaded?
 Ⓐ 40%
 Ⓑ 60%
 Ⓒ 30%
 Ⓓ 50%

20. What letter goes in the box to make this number sentence true?
 $(a \times b) \times c = a \times (\square \times c)$
 Ⓐ b
 Ⓑ a
 Ⓒ x
 Ⓓ c

STOP

STOP

Test 9: Mathematics Concepts/Applications: Reading Charts and Graphs (Form B)

Directions For questions 1–10 darken the circle for the correct answer.

Sample

What percent of the students in this school prefer to play volleyball?

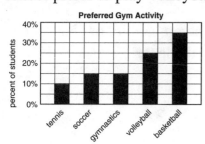

Preferred Gym Activity

- Ⓐ 35%
- Ⓑ 25%
- Ⓒ 40%
- Ⓓ 20%

Time: 15 minutes

For questions 1–3 use the information in the graph.

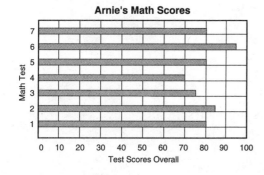

Arnie's Math Scores

1. On which tests did Arnie get more than 80%?
   - Ⓐ 2 and 5
   - Ⓑ 1 and 2
   - Ⓒ 2 and 6
   - Ⓓ 6 and 7

2. On which test did Arnie get the lowest score?
   - Ⓐ 4
   - Ⓑ 3
   - Ⓒ 1
   - Ⓓ 5

3. What is the second highest test score that Arnie earned?
   - Ⓐ 95
   - Ⓑ 80
   - Ⓒ 85
   - Ⓓ 75

Use the grid to answer questions 4–5.

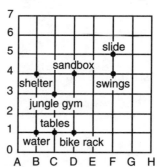

4. Which ordered pair shows the location of swings?
   - Ⓐ D, 4
   - Ⓑ C, 3
   - Ⓒ E, 5
   - Ⓓ F, 4

5. Which ordered pair shows the location of tables?
   - Ⓐ C, 2
   - Ⓑ C, 1
   - Ⓒ C, 3
   - Ⓓ D, 1

GO ON ⇨

Test 9: Mathematics Concepts/Applications: Reading Charts and Graphs (Form B), page 2

Use the graph to answer questions 6–7.

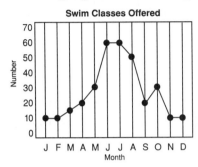

Swim Classes Offered

6. How many students took swimming classes in November and December?

Ⓐ 10 students

Ⓑ 20 students

Ⓒ 40 students

Ⓓ 15 students

7. In which two months did 30 students take swim classes?

Ⓐ April and May

Ⓑ May and September

Ⓒ September and October

Ⓓ May and October

Use the graph to answer questions 8–10.

Favorite Subject for Fifth-Grade Students

Science	📖📖📖
Social Studies	📖📖📖📖📖📖
Math	📖📖📖📖📖📖📖📖📖
Language	📖📖📖📖📖📖📖📖

Each 📖 = 5 students

8. How many students chose language as their favorite subject?

Ⓐ 40 students

Ⓑ 8 students

Ⓒ 20 students

Ⓓ 50 students

9. How many more students like math better than science?

Ⓐ 45 students

Ⓑ 15 students

Ⓒ 30 students

Ⓓ 25 students

10. A graph used to show changes by connecting dots is called _____ .

Ⓐ a pictograph

Ⓑ a circle graph

Ⓒ a bar graph

Ⓓ a line graph

STOP

STOP

Test 10: Mathematics Problem-Solving (Form A)

Directions For questions 1–40 darken the circle for the correct answer.

Sample A

Wanda is saving her money for a trip next summer. By the end of last week, she had saved $76. She had earned $35 for baby-sitting. Yesterday she bought a new T-shirt for $15. How much money did she have in her savings before last week?

What strategy should you use to solve this problem?

Ⓐ Identify extra information

Ⓑ Choose an operation

Ⓒ Make a chart

Ⓓ Work backwards

Sample B

If there are 40 problems on an exam that has a time limit of 20 minutes, how many problems must you do in one minute?

Ⓐ 2

Ⓑ 10

Ⓒ 4

Ⓓ 1

Time: 45 minutes

1. Dale is planning to make gifts for his family. He needs to buy craft supplies for all the gifts. He spent $5 for yarn the first day he went shopping, $8 for beads the next day, and $6 for ribbons on the third day. If he continues to spend money this way, about how much will he spend in a week?

   What strategy should you use to solve this problem?

Ⓐ Make a table

Ⓑ Find a pattern

Ⓒ Make a graph

Ⓓ Choose the operation

2. Gemella bought a blouse as a gift for Sonia. She is sharing the cost of the gift with her friend Rosie. She can't find the receipt, so she doesn't know exactly how much Rosie owes her. She knows that she paid for the blouse with a twenty-dollar bill. What else does she need to know in order to know exactly how much money she spent?

Ⓐ the color of the blouse

Ⓑ how much change she received

Ⓒ the name of the store

Ⓓ the size of the blouse

3. There were 6,008 books in the village library last year. After new books were purchased, they had 6,695 books. How many new books were added?

Ⓐ 687 books

Ⓑ 12,113 books

Ⓒ 695 books

Ⓓ 87 books

4. The ball park has 47 rows in the bleachers. Each row has 98 seats. What is the best way to estimate how many people can sit in the bleachers?

Ⓐ 47×98

Ⓑ 50×100

Ⓒ 40×90

Ⓓ 45×95

GO ON ⇨

Test 10: Mathematics Problem-Solving
(Form A), page 2

5. How much would it cost to carpet a room that is 18 feet long and 15 feet wide if the carpet costs $18.50 a square yard?

What strategy should you use to solve this problem?

Ⓐ Guess and check

Ⓑ Choose the operation

Ⓒ Use a multi-step plan

Ⓓ Make a graph

6. Sarah is planning to give a party. She will invite 15 people. She figures that a cake will cost $16 and cheese, crackers, and punch will cost $14. How much will Sarah spend for each guest?

Ⓐ $14

Ⓑ $16

Ⓒ $30

Ⓓ $2

7. Manuel and his friends are giving out flyers for a local supermarket. They have 1,000 flyers to give out. They plan to divide the flyers into stacks containing 50 flyers each. To find how many stacks each person will have, what do you need to know?

Ⓐ how many houses they will have to go to

Ⓑ how many friends will be distributing the flyers

Ⓒ what streets they will go to

Ⓓ where the local supermarket is located

8. A recipe calls for $2\frac{1}{4}$ cups of flour. The recipe makes eight servings. How many cups of flour will be needed to make 24 servings?

What strategy should you use to solve this problem?

Ⓐ Work backwards

Ⓑ Use a multi-step plan

Ⓒ Guess and check

Ⓓ Make a pattern

9. The Jefferson School held a walkathon to raise money for their media center. The goal was to raise $700. The total amount raised was $847.56. By how much did they go over their goal?

Ⓐ $147.56

Ⓑ $1,547.56

Ⓒ $847.56

Ⓓ $700.00

10. Ms. Atkins' fourth-grade class raised $115.67. Mr. Ryan's fifth-grade class raised $27.93 more than the fourth-grade class. How much did the fifth grade raise?

Ⓐ $143.60

Ⓑ $27.93

Ⓒ $115.67

Ⓓ $87.74

GO ON ⇨

Test 10: Mathematics Problem-Solving (Form A), page 3

11. Ms. Rivera's sixth-grade class hoped to raise $135. They missed their goal by $8.62. How much money did Ms. Rivera's class raise?
    - Ⓐ $144.42
    - Ⓑ $135.00
    - Ⓒ $126.38
    - Ⓓ $127.28

12. Gloria pledged to walk 15 kilometers. She earned $1.10 per km for the first ten kilometers that she walked. She earned $1.18 per km for each kilometer over 10 km that she walked. How much did she earn for meeting her pledge?
    - Ⓐ $16.90
    - Ⓑ $5.90
    - Ⓒ $11.00
    - Ⓓ $16.50

13. Derek went to a card show and spent about $56 on baseball cards. He spent $17 on hockey cards. At the end of the day he had $37 left. How much money did he start out with?
    - Ⓐ $73
    - Ⓑ $147
    - Ⓒ $110
    - Ⓓ $39

14. Rodney collects miniature cars. Last week he bought some new models and doubled the number of cars he had on his shelf. His grandparents gave him 6 more cars. If Rodney now has 46 cars, how many did he start with?
    What strategy would you use to solve this problem?
    - Ⓐ Use guess and check
    - Ⓑ Work backwards
    - Ⓒ Make a list
    - Ⓓ Use a graph

15. Buddy's room is 12 feet long and 9 feet wide. How many yards long is Buddy's room?
    - Ⓐ 4 yards
    - Ⓑ 6 yards
    - Ⓒ 3 yards
    - Ⓓ 9 yards

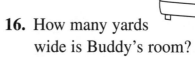

16. How many yards wide is Buddy's room?
    - Ⓐ 4 yards
    - Ⓑ 3 yards
    - Ⓒ 12 yards
    - Ⓓ 18 yards

17. If Buddy's parents put down a new floor in his room, how many square feet of flooring will they need?
    - Ⓐ 21 square feet
    - Ⓑ 108 square feet
    - Ⓒ 12 square feet
    - Ⓓ 120 square feet

GO ON ⇨

Test 10: Mathematics Problem-Solving (Form A), page 4

18. The Anderson family is planning to put a fence around their garden. The garden is 82 feet long and 36 feet wide. How much fencing will they need to go around the perimeter of the garden?

Ⓐ 164 feet

Ⓑ 72 feet

Ⓒ 118 feet

Ⓓ 236 feet

19. Adult tickets to the school play cost $3.50. Student tickets cost $1.75. On Saturday 426 student tickets and 342 adult tickets were sold. How much money did the school make?

What strategy should you use to solve this problem?

Ⓐ Choose an operation

Ⓑ Work backwards

Ⓒ Make a multi-step plan

Ⓓ Use estimation

20. Mimi and her friend are planning to visit Washington, D.C., for a three-day weekend. They estimate that they will each spend about $90.00 a day. About how much money will Mimi and her friend need altogether for the weekend?

Ⓐ $540

Ⓑ $270

Ⓒ $90

Ⓓ $180

21. Shane's hobby is photography. On his last camping trip, he took 2 rolls of 24-exposure film and 3 rolls of 36-exposure film. How many pictures did he take altogether?

Ⓐ 108 pictures

Ⓑ 48 pictures

Ⓒ 156 pictures

Ⓓ 60 pictures

22. Rudy bought a 36-exposure roll of film for $4.80. It cost him $6 to have the film developed. What was the average cost per picture?

Ⓐ $6

Ⓑ 30¢

Ⓒ 68¢

Ⓓ 80¢

23. Rosa wanted to walk around the school track 32 times. She stopped to rest after the 24th time. What percent of her goal did Rosa complete?

Ⓐ 25%

Ⓑ 80%

Ⓒ 75%

Ⓓ 90%

GO ON ⇒

Test 10: Mathematics Problem-Solving (Form A), page 5

24. Yvonne is making a new skirt to wear to the school dance. She will need $1\frac{1}{2}$ yards of fabric for the skirt and $\frac{3}{4}$ yard of ribbon for the trim. How much more fabric than ribbon trim does she need to buy?

    Ⓐ $\frac{1}{6}$ yard

    Ⓑ $\frac{3}{4}$ yard

    Ⓒ $\frac{1}{2}$ yard

    Ⓓ $\frac{1}{4}$ yard

25. Last month the students of Wingate School collected 657 empty soda cans for recycling. This month they collected 423 cans. How many cans did they collect for both months?

    Ⓐ 1,000 cans

    Ⓑ   234 cans

    Ⓒ 1,234 cans

    Ⓓ 1,080 cans

26. Jeanine is making bead necklaces as gifts. She made one necklace with 36 beads on it and another with 52 beads. Then she decided that both necklaces should have the same number of beads. She would take some beads off the larger necklace to add to the smaller necklace. How many beads would she have to take off the larger necklace in order for both necklaces to have an equal number of beads?

    Ⓐ   8 beads

    Ⓑ 16 beads

    Ⓒ 20 beads

    Ⓓ 18 beads

27. The school band decided to have a plant sale to raise money for new uniforms. The nursery charged them $4.95 for each flat of petunias and $3.95 for each flat of marigolds. The sales tax is 5.75%. What other information is needed to find the total cost of the plants?

    Ⓐ how many plants there are in a flat

    Ⓑ the color of the flowers in each flat

    Ⓒ how many flats they ordered

    Ⓓ how many flats each band member sold

28. Marie has 4 sets of flowered barrettes, 2 sets of pink barrettes, and 6 sets of silver barrettes. If she reaches into her barrette drawer without looking, what is the probability that she will pick a pair of flowered barrettes?

    Ⓐ 1:2

    Ⓑ 1:3

    Ⓒ 1:4

    Ⓓ 1:6

29. Ricky had $20.00 when he went to the mall last Saturday. He bought a gift for $6.95 and spent $4.89 on lunch. How much money did he still have when he went home?

    Ⓐ $7.00

    Ⓑ $6.18

    Ⓒ $5.29

    Ⓓ $8.16

GO ON ⇨

Test 10: Mathematics Problem-Solving (Form A), page 6

Read the problem. Then answer questions 30–31.

30. Vinnie rode his bike 1.2 miles round trip to and from the skating rink. It took him 20 minutes to ride each way. If he goes to the rink twice a week, how many miles in all will he ride? Which information don't you need to solve this problem?

Ⓐ It took him 20 minutes to ride each way.

Ⓑ He went to the rink twice a week.

Ⓒ He rode 1.2 miles to and from the rink.

Ⓓ He rode to a skating rink.

31. Use the information you need to solve the problem.

Ⓐ 1.2 miles

Ⓑ 2.4 miles

Ⓒ 2.0 miles

Ⓓ 4.8 miles

32. Zoe is preparing for a concert. She has six more days left to practice. She practiced 3 hours on Monday and 2 hours on Tuesday. What information do you need in order to find out how many hours Zoe practiced all week?

Ⓐ the names of the pieces she practiced

Ⓑ which day she didn't practice

Ⓒ how many hours she practiced on Wednesday, Thursday, Friday, and Saturday

Ⓓ what day the concert will take place

33. One day last month the school cafeteria sold 178 ice-cream cones. The next day it sold 212 ice-cream cones. How many ice-cream cones were sold altogether?

Ⓐ 400

Ⓑ 390

Ⓒ 350

Ⓓ 420

34. The sum of three consecutive numbers is 159. What are the three numbers? **What strategy should you use to solve this problem?**

Ⓐ Choose the operation

Ⓑ Guess and check

Ⓒ Find the pattern

Ⓓ Make a list

35. Attendance at the championship soccer game was 3,458. This total included 100 complimentary tickets that were given away. How many people paid for their tickets?

Ⓐ 3,358

Ⓑ 3,458

Ⓒ 3,558

Ⓓ 13,458

GO ON ⇨

Test 10: Mathematics Problem-Solving
(Form A), page 7

36. John's mother bought a 2-liter bottle of apple juice. John and his brothers drank 0.75 liters of juice. How much was left in the carton?

Ⓐ   1.25   liters
Ⓑ   12.5   liters
Ⓒ   1.025 liters
Ⓓ   1.205 liters

37. Apple pickers at Sweet Orchards picked 125 bushels of apples. Each bushel of apples weighed 75 pounds. How many pounds did they pick altogether?

Ⓐ   937 pounds
Ⓑ   90,375 pounds
Ⓒ   9,375 pounds
Ⓓ   93,750 pounds

38. Ian jumped $7\frac{1}{2}$ feet in the broad jump contest. Carlos jumped $6\frac{1}{4}$ feet. How much farther did Ian jump than Carlos?

Ⓐ $1\frac{1}{2}$ feet
Ⓑ $1\frac{1}{4}$ feet
Ⓒ $1\frac{3}{4}$ feet
Ⓓ $1\frac{1}{8}$ feet

39. If a year has 365 days and a day has 24 hours, how many hours are there in a year?

Ⓐ   7,860 hours
Ⓑ   6,780 hours
Ⓒ   8,670 hours
Ⓓ   8,760 hours

40. Ramona and her roommate signed a three-year lease for an apartment. Each of them will pay $220 a month for rent. How much money will Ramona have spent for rent by the time the lease is over?

Ⓐ $7,920.00
Ⓑ $790.20
Ⓒ $8,290.00
Ⓓ $79,200.00

STOP

STOP

Test 10: Mathematics Problem-Solving (Form B)

Directions For questions 1–40 darken the circle for the correct answer.

Sample A

Yoko, Ivy, and Lynda planned to meet at the library after school. One girl walked, one rode her bike, and the other skated. Lynda doesn't know how to skate. Ivy waved from her bike when she saw Lynda crossing the street. How did each girl get to the library?

What strategy should you use to solve this problem?

Ⓐ Make a list

Ⓑ Use estimation

Ⓒ Use logic

Ⓓ Choose an operation

Sample B

Valerie has 5 coins. Their total value is 47¢. What coins does Valerie have?

Ⓐ 4 dimes, 1 nickel

Ⓑ 1 quarter, 4 nickels

Ⓒ 1 quarter, 2 dimes, 2 pennies

Ⓓ 3 dimes, 1 quarter, 1 nickel

Time: 45 minutes

1. Leonard has $38 to spend on CDs and tapes. The tapes he wants cost $7.78 each. The CDs cost $9.98. Does he have enough money to buy 3 tapes and 2 CDs?

   What strategy should you use to solve this problem?

   Ⓐ Use estimation

   Ⓑ Work backwards

   Ⓒ Use logic

   Ⓓ Make a list

2. Karla painted a mural that is 8.06 meters long. Her friend Ray painted a mural that is 8.54 meters long. How much longer is Ray's mural than Karla's mural?

   Ⓐ 4.8 meters

   Ⓑ 48 meters

   Ⓒ 0.48 meters

   Ⓓ 4.08 meters

3. The Bonshaw River is about 180 kilometers long. French River is about 21 times as long. How long is French River?

   Ⓐ 378 kilometers

   Ⓑ 3,780 kilometers

   Ⓒ 7,803 kilometers

   Ⓓ 4,230 kilometers

4. Erica is using glittery stickers in the shape of stars and circles to decorate gift packages. She has 43 silver stars and 78 bronze circles. She bought 20 of the stars and 50 of the circles this morning. How many of each did she have before she went shopping today?

   Ⓐ 33 stars, 43 circles

   Ⓑ 35 stars, 50 circles

   Ⓒ 23 stars, 28 circles

   Ⓓ 27 stars, 28 circles

GO ON ⇨

Test 10: Mathematics Problem-Solving (Form B), page 2

5. Henry is in charge of serving punch at the school picnic. Each punch cup holds 245 milliliters. He needs to fill 14 punch cups. How much punch will he need?

Ⓐ 3,430 milliliters

Ⓑ 825 milliliters

Ⓒ 3,043 milliliters

Ⓓ 4,303 milliliters

Read the problem. Then answer questions 6–7.

6. There are 18 girls in a scout troop. For Mother's Day they are decorating baskets with lace and ribbons. Each girl needs 2 feet of ribbon to complete her project. The ribbon costs $0.39 per foot. How much will the ribbon cost for all the girls?

What strategy should you use to solve this problem?

Ⓐ Find a pattern

Ⓑ Make a list

Ⓒ Use a multi-step plan

Ⓓ Work backwards

7. Now solve the problem.

Ⓐ $14.04

Ⓑ $18.00

Ⓒ $3.90

Ⓓ $7.96

8. Anita wants to earn money to pay for her class trip in the spring. She plans to sell chocolate chip cookies. It costs her $2.10 to make one dozen cookies. She expects to sell the cookies for $3.50 a dozen. How much money will she make if she sells 12 dozen cookies?

Ⓐ $1.40

Ⓑ $16.80

Ⓒ $6.80

Ⓓ $12.40

9. The soccer team will have a three-day car wash to raise money. They will wash cars from 3:00 P.M. to 5:00 P.M. on Thursday and Friday. They will work from 10:00 A.M. to 4:00 P.M. on Saturday. How many hours in all will they be washing cars?

Ⓐ 8 hours

Ⓑ 12 hours

Ⓒ 10 hours

Ⓓ 14 hours

GO ON ⇨

Test 10: Mathematics Problem-Solving (Form B), page 3

10. Esther is filling 15 "loot bags" for her brother's birthday party. She will place 5 items inside each bag. How many items will she need to fill all the bags?
    - Ⓐ 25
    - Ⓑ 75
    - Ⓒ 20
    - Ⓓ 60

11. Admission to a theme park costs $24.50 per person. On Tuesdays the park has a special promotion that lets you buy a five-pack of tickets for $98. How much money would a family of five save if they went to the park on Tuesday?
    - Ⓐ $24.50
    - Ⓑ $2.00
    - Ⓒ $4.50
    - Ⓓ $22.50

12. Maida sells hand-knit hats for $46.95 each. Last week she sold 8 hats. What is the best estimate of how much money she earned for the hats?
    - Ⓐ $100
    - Ⓑ $200
    - Ⓒ $300
    - Ⓓ $400

13. There are 25 pencils in each of 5 boxes. How many pencils are there in all of the boxes?
    - Ⓐ 100
    - Ⓑ 121
    - Ⓒ 125
    - Ⓓ 50

14. Eleanor is older than Grace. Samantha is younger than Grace. Leona is older than Eleanor. Who is the oldest?
    - Ⓐ Eleanor
    - Ⓑ Grace
    - Ⓒ Samantha
    - Ⓓ Leona

Read the problem. Then answer questions 15–16.

15. The Allenwood School has 408 fiction books in the library. There are 219 biographies in the library. What operation should you use to find how many more fiction books than biography books the library has?
    - Ⓐ addition
    - Ⓑ subtraction
    - Ⓒ multiplication
    - Ⓓ division

16. How many books are there in all?
    - Ⓐ 617
    - Ⓑ 628
    - Ⓒ 619
    - Ⓓ 627

GO ON ⇨

Test 10: Mathematics Problem-Solving (Form B), page 4

17. Bus fare from Johnson City to Palmerville is $1.25. What do you need to know to find out if Vanessa and her friends can get from Johnson City to Palmerville with $10.00?

Ⓐ how many miles they have to go
Ⓑ what time of day they are going
Ⓒ how many of them will be going
Ⓓ how many stops the bus will make

18. Marcia's tennis game started at 4:30 P.M. She finished playing at 5:15 P.M. How long did her game last?

Ⓐ 45 minutes
Ⓑ 15 minutes
Ⓒ 30 minutes
Ⓓ 50 minutes

19. Michele sold 20, then 23, then 19, and then 26 tulip bulbs to four different families. What was the average number of bulbs she sold per family?

Ⓐ 88 bulbs
Ⓑ 4 bulbs
Ⓒ 22 bulbs
Ⓓ 36 bulbs

20. Laura used $\frac{3}{4}$ cup of milk for a pudding recipe, $\frac{1}{2}$ cup of milk for a cake recipe, and $\frac{1}{4}$ cup of milk for whipped potatoes. How many cups of milk did she use altogether?

Ⓐ $1\frac{1}{2}$ cups
Ⓑ $1\frac{3}{4}$ cups
Ⓒ $1\frac{1}{4}$ cups
Ⓓ $2\frac{1}{2}$ cups

21. Lizzie is counting the pennies in her piggy bank. When she counts by threes, she has one penny left. When she counts by eights, she has two pennies left. How many pennies does Lizzie have?

Ⓐ 34 pennies
Ⓑ 45 pennies
Ⓒ 26 pennies
Ⓓ 52 pennies

22. Mrs. Nichols gave her class 48 problems to do for homework. She also gave them 25 optional problems to do for extra credit. Drew did all of his homework and 15 of the optional problems. How many problems did Drew do?

Ⓐ 73
Ⓑ 58
Ⓒ 63
Ⓓ 40

Read the problem. Then answer questions 23–24.

23. Jill made a square using 4 toothpicks. She added 3 toothpicks to make two squares side by side. She made three squares in a row using 10 toothpicks. How many toothpicks would Jill need to make five squares in a row?
What strategy should be used to solve this problem?

Ⓐ Make a table
Ⓑ Make a graph
Ⓒ Find the pattern
Ⓓ Guess and check

GO ON ⇨

Test 10: Mathematics Problem-Solving
(Form B), page 5

24. Now solve the problem.
- Ⓐ 13 toothpicks
- Ⓑ 16 toothpicks
- Ⓒ 12 toothpicks
- Ⓓ 19 toothpicks

25. Sophie needs 12 ounces of cheese for a recipe. What fractional part of a pound does she need?
- Ⓐ $\frac{1}{4}$ pound
- Ⓑ $\frac{1}{2}$ pound
- Ⓒ $\frac{3}{4}$ pound
- Ⓓ $\frac{1}{3}$ pound

26. Jeremy's racing car can reach a top speed of 24.4 kilometers an hour. Charlie just got a new racing car that can go 2.8 times as fast as Jeremy's car. How fast can Charlie's car go per hour?
- Ⓐ 19.52 kilometers per hour
- Ⓑ 48.80 kilometers per hour
- Ⓒ 68.32 kilometers per hour
- Ⓓ 64.30 kilometers per hour

Read the problem. Then answer questions 27–28.

27. Mrs. Taylor and Mr. Flannigan are buying some new computer equipment for their school. They need 8 new printers at a cost of $315.50 each. They also need 15 ink cartridges at a cost of $21.06 each. What will the total cost of this equipment be?

What strategy should you use to solve this problem?
- Ⓐ Guess and check
- Ⓑ Find the extra information
- Ⓒ Estimate
- Ⓓ Use a multi-step plan

28. Now solve the problem.
- Ⓐ $2,524.00
- Ⓑ $315.90
- Ⓒ $2,539.90
- Ⓓ $2,839.90

29. A normal heart can pump 23.5 liters of blood through the body every five minutes. How many liters of blood can the heart pump in one minute?
- Ⓐ .04 liters
- Ⓑ 4.7 liters
- Ⓒ 47 liters
- Ⓓ 4.07 liters

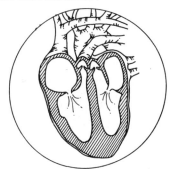

30. Sam and Ian went fishing. Sam caught a trout that weighed $3\frac{1}{2}$ pounds. Ian caught a trout that weighed $4\frac{1}{4}$ pounds. How much heavier is Ian's trout than Sam's?
- Ⓐ $\frac{3}{4}$ pound
- Ⓑ $1\frac{1}{2}$ pounds
- Ⓒ $\frac{1}{4}$ pound
- Ⓓ $\frac{1}{2}$ pound

GO ON ⇨

Test 10: Mathematics Problem-Solving
(Form B), page 6

31. The restaurant where Mario eats lunch sells vegetable soup with oyster crackers and potato soup with wheat crackers. How many different soup and cracker combinations can Mario choose from?

Ⓐ 3
Ⓑ 4
Ⓒ 8
Ⓓ 2

32. Olga used 6 yards of fabric to make 3 pillows. How many yards of the same fabric will she need to make 8 pillows?

Ⓐ 24 yards
Ⓑ 14 yards
Ⓒ 16 yards
Ⓓ 10 yards

33. The Nogales family spent $78 for souvenirs at an amusement park. T-shirts cost $18 and vests cost $15. They bought one T-shirt. How many vests did they buy?

Ⓐ 2 vests
Ⓑ 3 vests
Ⓒ 6 vests
Ⓓ 4 vests

34. Tanya bought 3 boxes of plant food for her African violets. Each box cost $0.75. How much did the plant food cost altogether?

Ⓐ $2.25
Ⓑ $2.10
Ⓒ $1.75
Ⓓ $1.50

35. Dora is 3 inches shorter than her cousin Mattie. What information do you need to have in order to find out how tall Dora is?

Ⓐ Dora's birthday
Ⓑ Mattie's height
Ⓒ Mattie's age
Ⓓ how many inches Dora grew last year

36. Alfonse rides his bike 8 miles each day when he delivers newspapers. So far this year he has gone 1,400 miles. How many days did he deliver newspapers?

Ⓐ 200 days
Ⓑ 175 days
Ⓒ 225 days
Ⓓ 165 days

37. Some friends saved their money to buy clothes. Felicia saved $45. Velma saved $30. When they went shopping, Felicia bought a sweater for $39. Velma didn't buy anything. How much money did Carol have left?

What strategy should you use to solve this problem?

Ⓐ Find a pattern
Ⓑ Identify missing information
Ⓒ Choose an operation
Ⓓ Make a table

GO ON ⇨

Test 10: Mathematics Problem-Solving
(Form B), page 7

38. Perry, Tim, and Jonas each have a younger child in their family. Together, the boys' families have two sisters and one brother. Tim doesn't have a sister. Which boys have sisters? Who has a brother?

What strategy should you use to solve this problem?

Ⓐ Use guess and check

Ⓑ Use estimation

Ⓒ Use logic

Ⓓ Find a pattern

39. The Jolly Chefs Club planned to sell hamburgers at the craft fair. They bought 5,184 buns that came in boxes of 12 per box. How many boxes of buns did they have?

Ⓐ 432 boxes

Ⓑ 300 boxes

Ⓒ 520 boxes

Ⓓ 624 boxes

40. Marcella's mother baked muffins and breads for the holiday. She used $1\frac{1}{2}$ pounds of nuts for both recipes. If she used $\frac{3}{4}$ pound of nuts for the muffins, how much did she use for the breads?

Ⓐ 1 pound

Ⓑ $\frac{1}{2}$ pound

Ⓒ $\frac{1}{4}$ pound

Ⓓ $\frac{3}{4}$ pound

STOP

STOP

Test 11: Study Skills (Form A)

Directions For questions 1–44 darken the circle for the correct answer.

Sample A

Which detail below fits best in line II-B?

Alexander Graham Bell

I. Life in Scotland
   A. _____
   B. Education
II. Bell the Inventor
   A. Earliest Inventions
   B. _____
   C. Later Work

Ⓐ Childhood
Ⓑ Most Famous Invention
Ⓒ Life on Cape Breton
Ⓓ Family Life

Sample B

In which chapter might you read about a trip to China?

Contents

Chapter
1. Men of the Nile
   by Enid L. Meadowcroft 58
2. Sea-Rovers of the North
   by Louise Dickinson Rich 64
3. The Tournament
   by Sean Morrison 71
4. Marco Polo's Great Adventure
   by Roger Duvoisin 79

Ⓐ Chapter 1
Ⓑ Chapter 2
Ⓒ Chapter 3
Ⓓ Chapter 4

Time: 45 minutes

GO ON ⇨

Test 11: Study Skills (Form A), page 2

Sample C

Which entry word belongs between the guide words *joyous/jury*?

(A) joyful

(B) junior

(C) journal

(D) just

Sample D

According to this map, what route should you take to go from Chandler to Cook?

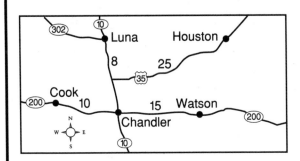

(A) Route 200 West

(B) Route 200 East

(C) Route 10 North

(D) Route 10 South

Look at this outline. Then answer questions 1–3.

Kinds of Sports

I. Team Sports
  A. Football
  B. _____
  C. Baseball
  D. Basketball

II. _____
  A. In-line Skating
  B. Canoeing
  C. _____
  D. Swimming

1. Which detail belongs on line I-B ?
  (A) Hiking
  (B) Cross-country skiing
  (C) Soccer
  (D) Walking

2. Which topic fits line II?
  (A) Water Sports
  (B) Sports To Do on Your Own
  (C) Indoor Sports
  (D) Winter Sports

3. Which detail belongs on line II-C?
  (A) Snowboarding
  (B) Hockey
  (C) Soccer
  (D) Relay Racing

GO ON ⇨

Test 11: Study Skills (Form A), page 3

4. Which entry word would *not* fit between the guide words *disinterested/displeasure*?
- Ⓐ dismal
- Ⓑ dispel
- Ⓒ disgust
- Ⓓ display

Use these dictionary entries to answer questions 5–8.

ceiling *n.*
1. The overhead inside lining or finish of a room. **2.** The greatest height to which an airplane can rise under certain conditions or at which it can still have a clear view of the Earth. **3.** The highest amount that may be legally charged for rent, goods, or services.

character *n.*
1. A mark, a sign, or a symbol, especially a written or printed one, such as a letter or figure. **2.** All the qualities that make a person or thing different from other persons or things; nature. **3.** Moral strength. **4.** A person in a story or a play. **5.** An odd or peculiar person.

cheap *adj.*
1. Of low cost or price; as, a *cheap* watch. **2.** Worth little; of inferior quality; as, to sell *cheap* goods at high prices. **3.** Lowered in one's own opinion; as, to feel *cheap*. **4.** *adv.* Dealing in low prices or inferior goods; at low cost.

5. In which of these sentences is definition 3 for the word *ceiling* used correctly?
- Ⓐ The ceiling has stars painted on it.
- Ⓑ The rent ceiling for that apartment was just raised.
- Ⓒ The ceiling was low because of the bad weather.
- Ⓓ We need a new ceiling light.

6. Which definition best matches the *italicized* word in this sentence?

I want to find a *cheap* pocketbook that I can use when I go to work.
- Ⓐ 1 (adj)
- Ⓑ 4 (adv)
- Ⓒ 2 (adj)
- Ⓓ 3 (adj)

7. Which definition of *character* means the way a person behaves?
- Ⓐ Definition 1
- Ⓑ Definition 2
- Ⓒ Definition 4
- Ⓓ Definition 5

8. In which of these sentences is definition 1 for the word *character* used correctly?
- Ⓐ He has a fine character.
- Ⓑ The character I liked best in that book was the clown.
- Ⓒ The vase had a strange character engraved on the bottom.
- Ⓓ Don't you think he's a strange character?

GO ON ⇨

Name _____   Date _____

Test 11: Study Skills (Form A), page 4

Use this map to answer questions 9–12.

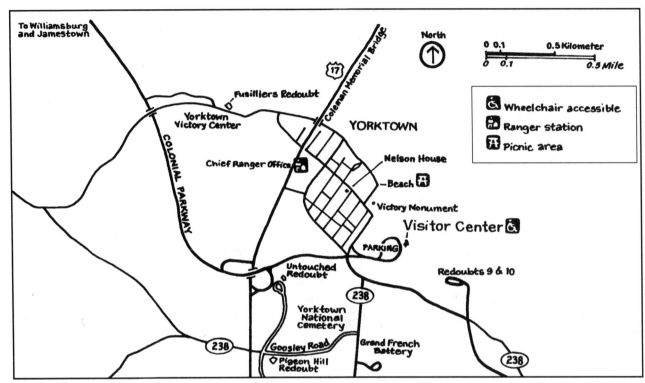

9. On what route is the Coleman
   Memorial Bridge?
   Ⓐ Route 238
   Ⓑ Route 17
   Ⓒ Route 704
   Ⓓ Route 637

10. Where will you find the Chief
    Ranger Office?
    Ⓐ at the beach
    Ⓑ on Pigeon Hill Redoubt
    Ⓒ on Route 17
    Ⓓ in Nelson House

11. Where is the Victory Monument
    located?
    Ⓐ near the beach
    Ⓑ at the Chief Ranger Station
    Ⓒ on Colonial Parkway
    Ⓓ in the Visitor Center

12. What road should you take to get
    to Williamsburg?
    Ⓐ Goosley Road
    Ⓑ Route 238
    Ⓒ Colonial Parkway
    Ⓓ Route 17

GO ON ⇨

Name _____ Date _____

Test 11: Study Skills (Form A), page 5

Look at this Table of Contents. Then answer questions 13–17.

Contents

13. On what pages will you read about life in colonial times?
Ⓐ pages 83–84
Ⓑ pages 85–89
Ⓒ pages 90–94
Ⓓ pages 101–103

14. By reading the headings in these three chapters, you can guess that they will mostly be about ____.
Ⓐ World War II
Ⓑ The Vietnam War
Ⓒ The Civil War
Ⓓ The Revolutionary War

15. On what page will you start to read about the writing of the *Constitution*?
Ⓐ page 128
Ⓑ page 123
Ⓒ page 136
Ⓓ page 143

16. What does the word *conclusion* at the end of each chapter probably mean?
Ⓐ summary
Ⓑ index
Ⓒ end
Ⓓ opinion

17. On what page will you start to read about different sections, or regions, of the colonies?
Ⓐ page 85
Ⓑ page 101
Ⓒ page 90
Ⓓ page 105

GO ON ⇨

Test 11: Study Skills (Form A), page 6

Use this index to answer questions 18–22.

Index of Authors and Titles

Andrews, Roy Chapman, 160
Architecture, My Way of Life, 111
Ashabranner, Brent, 284

Bendick, Jeanne, 27
Breaking the Bees' Code, 22
Bring 'Em Back Alive, 211

Nathan, Dorothy, 33
New Way of Life for Africa, A, 284

Simon, Charlie May, 122
Sterne, Emma Gelders, 377
Stone, Edward Durell, 111
Storms, Nature's Powerhouses, 223
Story of Weights and Measures, The, 27

This Man Was Mother to a Duck, 16
Toscanini Gets His Start, 116
Tournament, The, 71
Tragedy of the Tar Pits, 160

18. Who is the author of *Architecture, My Way of Life*?
Ⓐ Emma Gelders Sterne
Ⓑ Edward Durell Stone
Ⓒ Roy Chapman Andrews
Ⓓ Jeanne Bendick

19. What is the first word in the title of the book by Jeanne Bendick?
Ⓐ *Story*
Ⓑ *Weights*
Ⓒ *The*
Ⓓ *Measures*

20. What book did Brent Ashabranner write?
Ⓐ *Storms, Nature's Powerhouses*
Ⓑ *Architecture, My Way of Life*
Ⓒ *A New Way of Life for Africa*
Ⓓ *The Tournament*

21. Who is the author of *Tragedy of the Tar Pits*?
Ⓐ Dorothy Nathan
Ⓑ Roy Chapman Andrews
Ⓒ Edward Durell Stone
Ⓓ Jeanne Bendick

22. Who is the author of *The Story of Weights and Measures*?
Ⓐ Charlie May Simon
Ⓑ Brent Ashabranner
Ⓒ Jeanne Bendick
Ⓓ Emma Gelders Sterne

GO ON ⇨

Name _____ Date _____

Test 11: Study Skills (Form A), page 7

Use this street map to answer questions 23–27.

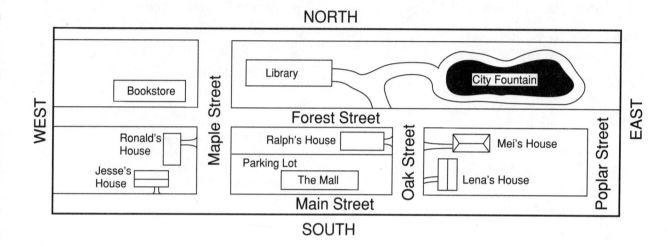

23. On what street can you find Lena's house?
   Ⓐ Oak Street
   Ⓑ Poplar Street
   Ⓒ Maple Street
   Ⓓ Forest Street

24. Where is Jesse's house?
   Ⓐ north of Maple Street
   Ⓑ north of Forest Street
   Ⓒ west of Maple Street
   Ⓓ east of Oak Street

25. Where is the parking lot located?
   Ⓐ behind the mall
   Ⓑ behind the library
   Ⓒ in front of the library
   Ⓓ on Poplar Street

26. What direction should Lena take to go from home to the library?
   Ⓐ southeast
   Ⓑ southwest
   Ⓒ northeast
   Ⓓ northwest

27. How many houses face onto Oak Street?
   Ⓐ 3 houses
   Ⓑ 2 houses
   Ⓒ 1 house
   Ⓓ 4 houses

GO ON ⇒

Test 11: Study Skills (Form A), page 8

Use this chart to answer questions 28–32.

Rare Coin Collection Record

Reggie	June	July	Aug.	Sept.
Pennies	28	93	86	43
Dimes	12	15	12	18
Len	**June**	**July**	**Aug.**	**Sept.**
Pennies	14	21	15	14
Dimes	35	24	24	51

28. In which month did Len collect 65 coins?
 Ⓐ June
 Ⓑ July
 Ⓒ August
 Ⓓ September

29. In which month did Reggie collect the most pennies?
 Ⓐ June
 Ⓑ July
 Ⓒ August
 Ⓓ September

30. In which month did both boys combined collect 47 dimes?
 Ⓐ June
 Ⓑ July
 Ⓒ August
 Ⓓ September

31. In which month did Len collect 15 pennies?
 Ⓐ June
 Ⓑ July
 Ⓒ August
 Ⓓ September

32. In which month did Reggie collect 15 dimes?
 Ⓐ June
 Ⓑ July
 Ⓒ August
 Ⓓ September

GO ON ⇨

Test 11: Study Skills (Form A), page 9

33. Where would you look to find out about the history of railroads in the United States?
Ⓐ an encyclopedia
Ⓑ an atlas
Ⓒ a thesaurus
Ⓓ a magazine

34. Where would you look to find out about weather conditions in a country you plan to visit next summer?
Ⓐ a science book
Ⓑ a newspaper
Ⓒ an almanac
Ⓓ an appendix

35. Where would you look to find out how to pronounce a word?
Ⓐ an encyclopedia
Ⓑ a dictionary
Ⓒ a thesaurus
Ⓓ an atlas

36. Where would you look to find the name of the capital of a state?
Ⓐ an atlas
Ⓑ the *Reader's Guide to Periodical Literature*
Ⓒ a science book
Ⓓ an almanac

37. Which key word in an index should you use to find out about Mozart, Beethoven, Brahms, and Bach?
Ⓐ Artists
Ⓑ Performers
Ⓒ Composers
Ⓓ Architects

38. Where would you find a call number?
Ⓐ in a card catalog
Ⓑ in a dictionary
Ⓒ in an encyclopedia
Ⓓ in an atlas

GO ON ⇨

Test 11: Study Skills (Form A), page 10

39. Where would you look to find the birth dates of famous people?
- Ⓐ in a magazine
- Ⓑ in a thesaurus
- Ⓒ in an almanac
- Ⓓ in an appendix

40. Which would have information on a new science discovery?
- Ⓐ *Life Magazine*
- Ⓑ *People*
- Ⓒ *Scientific American*
- Ⓓ *Prevention*

41. What does the number 796.323 on a card in the card catalog stand for?
- Ⓐ the year a book was published
- Ⓑ the number of books the author has written
- Ⓒ the number of pages in the book
- Ⓓ the call number for the book

42. What kind of information is found in a bibliography?
- Ⓐ the books an author used to get information
- Ⓑ the titles of other books the author has written
- Ⓒ the table of contents
- Ⓓ the glossary

43. What kind of information is found in a glossary?
- Ⓐ a list of maps
- Ⓑ the index
- Ⓒ special words found in a particular book
- Ⓓ special pictures and charts found in a particular book

44. What does an illustrator do?
- Ⓐ edits a book
- Ⓑ draws pictures for a book
- Ⓒ chooses photographs for a book
- Ⓓ copyrights a book

STOP

Test 11: Study Skills (Form B)

Directions For questions 1–48 darken the circle for the correct answer.

Sample A

Which detail fits in II-B?

Transportation

I. Air Transportation
  A. Jet Planes
  B. Helicopter
II. Ground Transportation
  A. Automobile
  B. _____
  C. Bus

Ⓐ Ferry
Ⓑ Sailboat
Ⓒ Train
Ⓓ Air Bus

Sample B

Contents

On what page will you learn how to take care of the printer safely?

Ⓐ page 6
Ⓑ page 3
Ⓒ page 1
Ⓓ page 2

Sample C

Which entry word fits between the guide words *build/bulwark*?

Ⓐ bulletin
Ⓑ bugle
Ⓒ bubble
Ⓓ buffet

Sample D

According to this map, on which side of the Muleshoe River is the city of Leander?

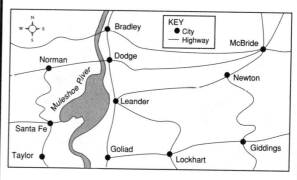

Ⓐ north
Ⓑ south
Ⓒ east
Ⓓ west

Time: 50 minutes

GO ON ⇨

Test 11: Study Skills (Form B), page 2

Look at this outline. Then answer questions 1–3.

I.   Books about dogs
    A. Dog varieties
    B. _____
    C. Caring for dogs
II. Dogs' needs
    A. Food
    B. Exercise
    C. _____
III. _____
    A. Scotties
    B. Collies
    C. Terriers

1. What would be a good title for this report?
   Ⓐ Friendly Dogs
   Ⓑ Good Watchdogs
   Ⓒ Dogs as Pets
   Ⓓ Working Dogs

2. Which detail belongs in II-C?
   Ⓐ Grooming
   Ⓑ Names
   Ⓒ Tricks
   Ⓓ Collars

3. Which topic belongs on line III?
   Ⓐ Small dogs
   Ⓑ Large dogs
   Ⓒ Hunting dogs
   Ⓓ Some dog varieties

4. Which entry word does *not* fit between the guide words *scale/scarlet*?
   Ⓐ scatter
   Ⓑ scalp
   Ⓒ scar
   Ⓓ scant

GO ON ⇨

Test 11: Study Skills (Form B), page 3

Use these dictionary entries to answer questions 5–8.

equal *adj.*
1. Exactly the same in number, amount, degree, rank, or quality; as, an *equal* number of apples and oranges; officers of *equal* rank. **2.** Evenly balanced; as, an *equal* contest. **3.** Having enough strength, ability, or means; adequate; as, to be *equal* to a difficult task. *-n.* A person or a thing that is equal to another. *-v.* **equaled** or **equalled; equaling** or **equalling.** To be or become equal to; to match.

order *n.*
1. A group of people united in some way, as by obeying the same rules, by working for the same purpose, or by having the same social position; as, an *order* of monks; a fraternal or military *order;* people from every *order* of society. **2.** The way things are, or happen to come about; as, the *order* of the seasons. **3.** A regular or harmonious arrangement; a system; as, in alphabetical *order;* a room that is in good *order.* **4.** General peace and quiet; as, to keep *order* in the classroom. **5.** A command, rule, or direction; as, to obey *orders.* **6.** A written direction or command. *-v.* **1.** To govern, direct, or command; as, to *order* troops to attack. **2.** To give an order for; as, to *order* something through the mail.

5. Which definition of *equal* is used in this sentence?
   The recipe calls for an equal amount of butter and cheese.
   Ⓐ Definition (verb)
   Ⓑ Definition 1 (adj)
   Ⓒ Definition 2 (adj)
   Ⓓ Definition 3 (adj)

6. If you are told to line up in size or place order, which definition of *order* is meant?
   Ⓐ Definition 5
   Ⓑ Definition 2
   Ⓒ Definition 3
   Ⓓ Definition 6

7. Which of these guide words would be on the same dictionary page as *order?*
   Ⓐ onwards/opposite
   Ⓑ opposition/order
   Ⓒ orderly/original
   Ⓓ originality/ourselves

8. If you *order* something from a catalog, which definition of the word are you using?
   Ⓐ Definition 2 (verb)
   Ⓑ Definition 2 (noun)
   Ⓒ Definition 1 (noun)
   Ⓓ Definition 1 (verb)

GO ON ⇨

Test 11: Study Skills (Form B), page 4

Look at this farm plan. Then answer questions 9–12.

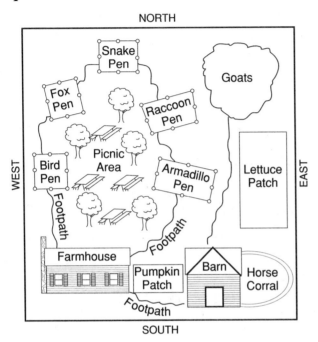

9. What will you pass if you go from the barn to the goat area?
   Ⓐ Pumpkin Patch
   Ⓑ Bird Pen
   Ⓒ Snake Pen
   Ⓓ Lettuce Patch

10. How many pens are there around the picnic area?
    Ⓐ four
    Ⓑ two
    Ⓒ five
    Ⓓ six

11. In what direction should you walk from the barn to get to the Horse Corral?
    Ⓐ east
    Ⓑ west
    Ⓒ north
    Ⓓ south

12. Where will you find the Raccoon Pen?
    Ⓐ between the Farmhouse and the Bird Pen
    Ⓑ between the Farmhouse and the Barn
    Ⓒ between the Armadillo Pen and the Snake Pen
    Ⓓ between the Horse Corral and the Lettuce Patch

GO ON ⇨

Test 11: Study Skills (Form B), page 5

Use the Table of Contents to answer questions 13–17.

Contents

13. From the table of contents, you can guess that this book is about what?
Ⓐ getting a job
Ⓑ doing well in school
Ⓒ getting along with others
Ⓓ writing good book reports

14. Which chapter tells about using your memory?
Ⓐ Chapter 1
Ⓑ Chapter 6
Ⓒ Chapter 5
Ⓓ Chapter 3

15. How many pages teach you ways to tackle your homework?
Ⓐ 14 pages
Ⓑ 15 pages
Ⓒ 18 pages
Ⓓ 10 pages

16. Which chapter teaches you how to take notes?
Ⓐ Chapter 6
Ⓑ Chapter 3
Ⓒ Chapter 2
Ⓓ Chapter 1

17. On what page does the chapter on taking tests begin?
Ⓐ page 77
Ⓑ page 31
Ⓒ page 1
Ⓓ page 17

GO ON ⇨

Test 11: Study Skills (Form B), page 6

Use this index to answer questions 18–23.

Index

Asia: famous mountains of, 179;
  mountain belts of, 12; map, 44–45
Atlantic Ocean, 39; volcanoes, 57, 61
Atlas Mountains, 12, 37, 44, 119, 134
Atmospheric pressure, 36, 131
Azores Islands, 57
Bighorn sheep, 109, 110, 119
Birds, 39, 108, 114–115
Bumblebee, 116
Cable cars, 23
Canadian Rockies, 48, 130
Catskills, 39, 137
Cinder cones, 52, 58–59, 68
Cirques, 14, 24
Death Valley, 36
Dipper, 115, 126
Douglas fir, 83

18. How many pages have information
    about bighorn sheep?
    Ⓐ three pages
    Ⓑ two pages
    Ⓒ four pages
    Ⓓ one page

19. If you read pages 58–59, what will you
    be reading about?
    Ⓐ Dipper
    Ⓑ Canadian Rockies
    Ⓒ Cinder cones
    Ⓓ Cirques

20. What will you read about on page 44?
    Ⓐ Mountain belts
    Ⓑ Volcanoes
    Ⓒ Atlas Mountains
    Ⓓ Death Valley

21. On what pages will you find a map
    of Asian mountains?
    Ⓐ pages 179–180
    Ⓑ pages 12–13
    Ⓒ pages 37–38
    Ⓓ pages 44–45

22. On what page will you find information
    about volcanoes in the Atlantic Ocean?
    Ⓐ page 39
    Ⓑ page 58
    Ⓒ page 61
    Ⓓ page 60

23. What subtopic is listed with famous
    mountains of Asia?
    Ⓐ Atlas Mountains
    Ⓑ Mountain belts in Asia
    Ⓒ Canadian Rockies
    Ⓓ Death Valley

GO ON ⇨

Test 11: Study Skills (Form B), page 7

Answer questions 24–28 about writing reports.

24. Which of these report-writing steps comes first?
    Ⓐ Write an outline
    Ⓑ Locate information
    Ⓒ Select a topic
    Ⓓ Write a report

25. If you want to write a report on how dogs help people, which of these topics would be the best to use?
    Ⓐ Dogs
    Ⓑ Good food for dogs
    Ⓒ Dog grooming
    Ⓓ Seeing-eye dogs

26. What do you think about the suitability of this topic for a report?
    Homes people have built since early times
    Ⓐ not enough information available
    Ⓑ topic too small
    Ⓒ topic too large
    Ⓓ suitable topic

27. What do you think about the suitability of this topic for a report?
    Gold-medal Olympic track winners in the eighties and nineties
    Ⓐ suitable topic
    Ⓑ topic too small
    Ⓒ topic too large
    Ⓓ not enough information available

28. If you were writing a report about Charles Lindbergh, which of these facts about his life would come first in the report?
    Ⓐ flew nonstop across the Atlantic
    Ⓑ went to flying school when he was 18 years old
    Ⓒ named his plane "Spirit of St. Louis"
    Ⓓ decided to try for $25,000 prize

GO ON ⇨

Test 11: Study Skills (Form B), page 8

> 910.4   Great railway journeys of the world /
> G   Michael Frayn .... [et al.]. – New York:
>   Dutton, ©1982.
>   182 p. : ill., maps ; 23 cm.
>   Includes index.
>   ISBN: 0-525-24152-3
>
>   1. Railroads.   2. Voyages and
>   travels. I. Frayn, Michael.
>
>   NL208A   82-71251

Use the catalog card to answer questions 29–34.

29. What kind of catalog card is this?
    - Ⓐ subject card
    - Ⓑ title card
    - Ⓒ author card
    - Ⓓ library card

30. How many pages are in this book?
    - Ⓐ 910 pages
    - Ⓑ 208 pages
    - Ⓒ 23 pages
    - Ⓓ 182 pages

31. Who is the publisher of this book?
    - Ⓐ Dutton
    - Ⓑ Michael Frayn
    - Ⓒ ISBN
    - Ⓓ Voyages

32. What is the call number for this book?
    - Ⓐ 523
    - Ⓑ 1982
    - Ⓒ 82
    - Ⓓ 910.4

33. Who is the main author of this book?
    - Ⓐ et al.
    - Ⓑ Michael Frayn
    - Ⓒ Great Railway Journeys
    - Ⓓ New York Dutton

34. What subject will be on the subject card?
    - Ⓐ Railroads
    - Ⓑ Frayn
    - Ⓒ New York
    - Ⓓ World

GO ON ⇨

Test 11: Study Skills (Form B), page 9

```
FIC         Morrell, David.
Morrell         Assumed identity / David Morrell.
            - - New York : Warner Books, ©1993.
            p.  cm.

            ISBN 0-446-51669-4

            1.    Spies — United States — Fiction.
            2.    Spies — Mexico — Fiction.
            I.    Title.
                                    92-51040
                                    AACR2 CIP
Library of Congress
005067   48-929-04   531056   ME        3240
```

Use this catalog card to answer questions 35–37.

35. What kind of book is this?
    Ⓐ fiction
    Ⓑ science fiction
    Ⓒ nonfiction
    Ⓓ social studies

36. What is the title of this book?
    Ⓐ *Spies*
    Ⓑ *United States*
    Ⓒ *Mexico*
    Ⓓ *Assumed Identity*

37. Who is the publisher of this book?
    Ⓐ David Morrell
    Ⓑ Warner Books
    Ⓒ Library of Congress
    Ⓓ AACR2 CIP

38. Where would you look to find out when a book was first published?
    Ⓐ appendix
    Ⓑ glossary
    Ⓒ copyright page
    Ⓓ introduction

39. Where would you look to find out about recent articles on vacation travel?
    Ⓐ *Book of Knowledge*
    Ⓑ the card catalog
    Ⓒ *Reader's Guide to Periodical Literature*
    Ⓓ an atlas

40. Where would you look to find the name of the publisher of a book?
    Ⓐ preface
    Ⓑ copyright page
    Ⓒ bibliography
    Ⓓ table of contents

GO ON ⇨

Name _____ Date _____

Test 11: Study Skills (Form B), page 10

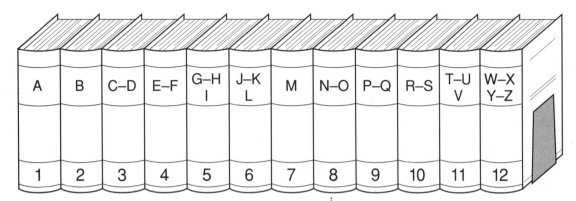

A	B	C–D	E–F	G–H I	J–K L	M	N–O	P–Q	R–S	T–U V	W–X Y–Z
1	2	3	4	5	6	7	8	9	10	11	12

Use this set of encyclopedias to answer questions 41–43.

41. Which encyclopedia volume would you use if you were writing a report on Italy?
(A) Volume 3
(B) Volume 8
(C) Volume 1
(D) Volume 5

42. Which encyclopedia volume would you use if you were writing a report on Russia?
(A) Volume 8
(B) Volume 9
(C) Volume 10
(D) Volume 11

43. Which encyclopedia volume would you use if you were writing a report on New Zealand?
(A) Volume 3
(B) Volume 8
(C) Volume 5
(D) Volume 12

44. Where would you look to find out how a word is pronounced?
(A) index
(B) dictionary
(C) atlas
(D) preface

GO ON ⇨

Test 11: Study Skills (Form B), page 11

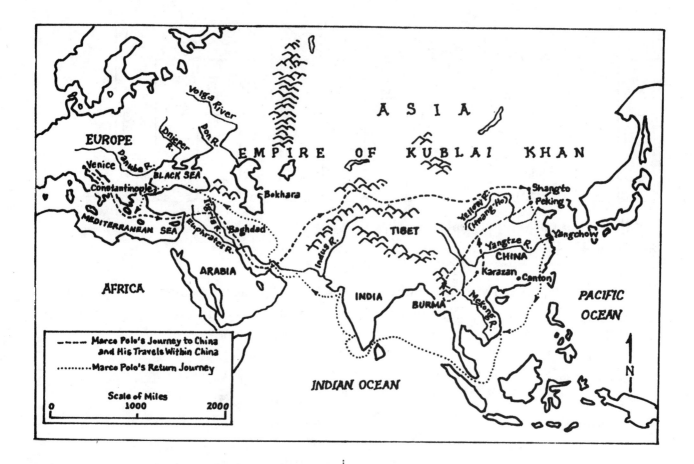

Use this map to answer questions 45–48.

45. From which city did Marco Polo start his journey to China?

- Ⓐ Constantinople
- Ⓑ Baghdad
- Ⓒ Venice
- Ⓓ Danube

46. What is the Chinese name for the Yellow River?

- Ⓐ Yangtze
- Ⓑ Hwang-Ho
- Ⓒ Karazan
- Ⓓ Shangto

47. From which city did Marco Polo start his return journey?

- Ⓐ Peking
- Ⓑ Yangchow
- Ⓒ Canton
- Ⓓ Bokhara

48. Which of these rivers is not in China?

- Ⓐ Yangtze
- Ⓑ Mekong
- Ⓒ Yellow
- Ⓓ Danube

STOP

STOP

STUDENT'S NAME		SCHOOL:
LAST	FIRST · MI	TEACHER:

FEMALE ○   MALE ○

BIRTH DATE

MONTH	DAY	YEAR
Jan ○	⓪ ⓪	⓪ ⓪
Feb ○	① ①	① ①
Mar ○	② ②	② ②
Apr ○	③ ③	③ ③
May ○	④	④ ④
Jun ○	⑤	⑤ ⑤
Jul ○	⑥	⑥ ⑥
Aug ○	⑦	⑦ ⑦
Sep ○	⑧	⑧ ⑧
Oct ○	⑨	⑨ ⑨
Nov ○		
Dec ○		

GRADE ② ③ ④ ⑤ ⑥

TEST PRACTICE GRADE 5
© Steck-Vaughn Company

(Name grid columns: Ⓐ Ⓑ Ⓒ Ⓓ Ⓔ Ⓕ Ⓖ Ⓗ Ⓘ Ⓙ Ⓚ Ⓛ Ⓜ Ⓝ Ⓞ Ⓟ Ⓠ Ⓡ Ⓢ Ⓣ Ⓤ Ⓥ Ⓦ Ⓧ Ⓨ Ⓩ)

Test 1: Vocabulary (Form) A B Part One

SA, 1–6, 7–12 & SB, SC, 13–18, 19–24 & SD, 25–28 — each with Ⓐ Ⓑ Ⓒ Ⓓ

Part Two

SA1, SA2, 1–6, SB, 7–9, 10–13, 14–16 — each with Ⓐ Ⓑ Ⓒ Ⓓ

Test 2: Reading Comprehension (Form) A B

S1, S2, 1–8, 9–18, 19–28, 29–38, 39–45 — each with Ⓐ Ⓑ Ⓒ Ⓓ

Test 3: Spelling (Form) A B

SA, 1–4, 5–9, 10, SB, 11–13, 14–18, 19–20 — each with Ⓐ Ⓑ Ⓒ Ⓓ

Test 3: Usage (Form) A B

SA, 1–7, 8–14, SB, 15–21, SC, 22–28, SD, 29–34 — each with Ⓐ Ⓑ Ⓒ Ⓓ

Test 4: Language Expression (Form) A B

	(A) (B) (C) (D)		(A) (B) (C) (D)		(A) (B) (C) (D)		(A) (B) (C) (D)		(A) (B) (C) (D)
SA	(A) (B) (C) (D)	1.	(A) (B) (C) (D)	4.	(A) (B) (C) (D)	7.	(A) (B) (C) (D)	10.	(A) (B) (C) (D)
		2.	(A) (B) (C) (D)	5.	(A) (B) (C) (D)	8.	(A) (B) (C) (D)	11.	(A) (B) (C) (D)
		3.	(A) (B) (C) (D)	6.	(A) (B) (C) (D)	9.	(A) (B) (C) (D)	12.	(A) (B) (C) (D)

Test 5: Mathematics Computation (Form) A B

SA	(A) (B) (C) (D)	6.	(A) (B) (C) (D)	15.	(A) (B) (C) (D)	24.	(A) (B) (C) (D)	33.	(A) (B) (C) (D)
SB	(A) (B) (C) (D)	7.	(A) (B) (C) (D)	16.	(A) (B) (C) (D)	25.	(A) (B) (C) (D)	34.	(A) (B) (C) (D)
SC	(A) (B) (C) (D)	8.	(A) (B) (C) (D)	17.	(A) (B) (C) (D)	26.	(A) (B) (C) (D)	35.	(A) (B) (C) (D)
SD	(A) (B) (C) (D)	9.	(A) (B) (C) (D)	18.	(A) (B) (C) (D)	27.	(A) (B) (C) (D)	36.	(A) (B) (C) (D)
1.	(A) (B) (C) (D)	10.	(A) (B) (C) (D)	19.	(A) (B) (C) (D)	28.	(A) (B) (C) (D)	37.	(A) (B) (C) (D)
2.	(A) (B) (C) (D)	11.	(A) (B) (C) (D)	20.	(A) (B) (C) (D)	29.	(A) (B) (C) (D)	38.	(A) (B) (C) (D)
3.	(A) (B) (C) (D)	12.	(A) (B) (C) (D)	21.	(A) (B) (C) (D)	30.	(A) (B) (C) (D)	39.	(A) (B) (C) (D)
4.	(A) (B) (C) (D)	13.	(A) (B) (C) (D)	22.	(A) (B) (C) (D)	31.	(A) (B) (C) (D)	40.	(A) (B) (C) (D)
5.	(A) (B) (C) (D)	14.	(A) (B) (C) (D)	23.	(A) (B) (C) (D)	32.	(A) (B) (C) (D)		

Test 6: Numeration/Number Theory (Form) A B

SA	(A) (B) (C) (D)	3.	(A) (B) (C) (D)	7.	(A) (B) (C) (D)	11.	(A) (B) (C) (D)	15.	(A) (B) (C) (D)
SB	(A) (B) (C) (D)	4.	(A) (B) (C) (D)	8.	(A) (B) (C) (D)	12.	(A) (B) (C) (D)	16.	(A) (B) (C) (D)
1.	(A) (B) (C) (D)	5.	(A) (B) (C) (D)	9.	(A) (B) (C) (D)	13.	(A) (B) (C) (D)	17.	(A) (B) (C) (D)
2.	(A) (B) (C) (D)	6.	(A) (B) (C) (D)	10.	(A) (B) (C) (D)	14.	(A) (B) (C) (D)	18.	(A) (B) (C) (D)

Test 7: Geometry/Measurement (Form) A B

SA	(A) (B) (C) (D)	1.	(A) (B) (C) (D)	4.	(A) (B) (C) (D)	7.	(A) (B) (C) (D)	10.	(A) (B) (C) (D)
SB	(A) (B) (C) (D)	2.	(A) (B) (C) (D)	5.	(A) (B) (C) (D)	8.	(A) (B) (C) (D)	11.	(A) (B) (C) (D)
		3.	(A) (B) (C) (D)	6.	(A) (B) (C) (D)	9.	(A) (B) (C) (D)	12.	(A) (B) (C) (D)

Test 8: Number Sentences/Ratios and Percents (Form) A B

SA	(A) (B) (C) (D)	4.	(A) (B) (C) (D)	9.	(A) (B) (C) (D)	14.	(A) (B) (C) (D)	19.	(A) (B) (C) (D)
SB	(A) (B) (C) (D)	5.	(A) (B) (C) (D)	10.	(A) (B) (C) (D)	15.	(A) (B) (C) (D)	20.	(A) (B) (C) (D)
1.	(A) (B) (C) (D)	6.	(A) (B) (C) (D)	11.	(A) (B) (C) (D)	16.	(A) (B) (C) (D)		
2.	(A) (B) (C) (D)	7.	(A) (B) (C) (D)	12.	(A) (B) (C) (D)	17.	(A) (B) (C) (D)		
3.	(A) (B) (C) (D)	8.	(A) (B) (C) (D)	13.	(A) (B) (C) (D)	18.	(A) (B) (C) (D)		

Test 9: Reading Charts and Graphs (Form) A B

S	(A) (B) (C) (D)	1.	(A) (B) (C) (D)	4.	(A) (B) (C) (D)	7.	(A) (B) (C) (D)	10.	(A) (B) (C) (D)
		2.	(A) (B) (C) (D)	5.	(A) (B) (C) (D)	8.	(A) (B) (C) (D)		
		3.	(A) (B) (C) (D)	6.	(A) (B) (C) (D)	9.	(A) (B) (C) (D)		

Test 10: Problem-Solving (Form) A B

SA	(A) (B) (C) (D)	8.	(A) (B) (C) (D)	17.	(A) (B) (C) (D)	26.	(A) (B) (C) (D)	35.	(A) (B) (C) (D)
SB	(A) (B) (C) (D)	9.	(A) (B) (C) (D)	18.	(A) (B) (C) (D)	27.	(A) (B) (C) (D)	36.	(A) (B) (C) (D)
1.	(A) (B) (C) (D)	10.	(A) (B) (C) (D)	19.	(A) (B) (C) (D)	28.	(A) (B) (C) (D)	37.	(A) (B) (C) (D)
2.	(A) (B) (C) (D)	11.	(A) (B) (C) (D)	20.	(A) (B) (C) (D)	29.	(A) (B) (C) (D)	38.	(A) (B) (C) (D)
3.	(A) (B) (C) (D)	12.	(A) (B) (C) (D)	21.	(A) (B) (C) (D)	30.	(A) (B) (C) (D)	39.	(A) (B) (C) (D)
4.	(A) (B) (C) (D)	13.	(A) (B) (C) (D)	22.	(A) (B) (C) (D)	31.	(A) (B) (C) (D)	40.	(A) (B) (C) (D)
5.	(A) (B) (C) (D)	14.	(A) (B) (C) (D)	23.	(A) (B) (C) (D)	32.	(A) (B) (C) (D)		
6.	(A) (B) (C) (D)	15.	(A) (B) (C) (D)	24.	(A) (B) (C) (D)	33.	(A) (B) (C) (D)		
7.	(A) (B) (C) (D)	16.	(A) (B) (C) (D)	25.	(A) (B) (C) (D)	34.	(A) (B) (C) (D)		

Test 11: Study Skills (Form) A B

SA	(A) (B) (C) (D)	8.	(A) (B) (C) (D)	19.	(A) (B) (C) (D)	30.	(A) (B) (C) (D)	41.	(A) (B) (C) (D)
SB	(A) (B) (C) (D)	9.	(A) (B) (C) (D)	20.	(A) (B) (C) (D)	31.	(A) (B) (C) (D)	42.	(A) (B) (C) (D)
SC	(A) (B) (C) (D)	10.	(A) (B) (C) (D)	21.	(A) (B) (C) (D)	32.	(A) (B) (C) (D)	43.	(A) (B) (C) (D)
SD	(A) (B) (C) (D)	11.	(A) (B) (C) (D)	22.	(A) (B) (C) (D)	33.	(A) (B) (C) (D)	44.	(A) (B) (C) (D)
1.	(A) (B) (C) (D)	12.	(A) (B) (C) (D)	23.	(A) (B) (C) (D)	34.	(A) (B) (C) (D)	45.	(A) (B) (C) (D)
2.	(A) (B) (C) (D)	13.	(A) (B) (C) (D)	24.	(A) (B) (C) (D)	35.	(A) (B) (C) (D)	46.	(A) (B) (C) (D)
3.	(A) (B) (C) (D)	14.	(A) (B) (C) (D)	25.	(A) (B) (C) (D)	36.	(A) (B) (C) (D)	47.	(A) (B) (C) (D)
4.	(A) (B) (C) (D)	15.	(A) (B) (C) (D)	26.	(A) (B) (C) (D)	37.	(A) (B) (C) (D)	48.	(A) (B) (C) (D)
5.	(A) (B) (C) (D)	16.	(A) (B) (C) (D)	27.	(A) (B) (C) (D)	38.	(A) (B) (C) (D)		
6.	(A) (B) (C) (D)	17.	(A) (B) (C) (D)	28.	(A) (B) (C) (D)	39.	(A) (B) (C) (D)		
7.	(A) (B) (C) (D)	18.	(A) (B) (C) (D)	29.	(A) (B) (C) (D)	40.	(A) (B) (C) (D)		

Test Practice Grade Five
Answer Key

P. 11–14
TEST 1: VOCABULARY-PART ONE, (FORM A)
SAMPLE A: B
1. A
2. C
3. B
4. A
5. A
6. C
7. B
8. D
SAMPLE B: A
9. B
10. A
11. C
12. B
13. D
14. A
15. B
16. D
SAMPLE C: B
17. B
18. A
19. C
20. D
21. B
22. D
SAMPLE D: D
23. C
24. B
25. A
26. C
27. D
28. A

P. 15–16
TEST 1: VOCABULARY-PART TWO (FORM A)
SAMPLE A: S1. C, S2. A
1. B
2. A
3. D
4. D
5. A
6. B
SAMPLE B: B
7. C
8. A
9. C
10. B
11. D
12. A
13. B
14. A
15. C
16. D

P. 17–20
TEST 1: VOCABULARY - PART ONE (FORM B)
SAMPLE A: B
1. A
2. C
3. A
4. C
5. B
6. C
7. B
8. A
SAMPLE B: A
9. A
10. C
11. A
12. B
13. D
14. C
15. A
16. B
SAMPLE C: D
17. C
18. D
19. B
20. D
21. B
22. D
SAMPLE D: D
23. B
24. A
25. C
26. B
27. A
28. C

P. 21–22
TEST 1: VOCABULARY-PART TWO (FORM B)
SAMPLE A: S1. A, S2. C
1. B
2. A
3. C
4. B
5. D
6. B
SAMPLE B: C
7. D
8. A
9. C
10. C
11. A
12. B
13. C
14. A
15. A
16. B

P. 23–33
TEST 2: READING COMPREHENSION (FORM A)
SAMPLE 1: C
SAMPLE 2: B
1. D
2. B
3. A
4. B
5. C
6. D
7. B
8. A
9. C
10. B
11. C
12. B
13. C
14. D
15. A
16. C
17. B
18. D
19. B
20. A
21. C
22. B
23. A
24. C
25. D
26. D
27. A
28. B
29. A
30. A
31. C
32. B
33. D
34. C
35. A
36. B
37. B
38. A
39. C
40. D
41. C
42. D
43. B
44. C
45. D

P. 34–45
TEST 2: READING COMPREHENSION (FORM B)
SAMPLE 1: C
SAMPLE 2: A
1. A
2. D
3. B
4. C
5. C
6. B
7. D
8. B
9. C
10. A
11. B
12. D
13. A
14. D
15. C
16. B
17. A
18. B
19. D
20. C
21. D
22. B
23. A
24. D
25. C
26. D
27. A
28. C
29. A
30. B
31. A
32. C
33. C
34. C
35. B
36. B
37. D
38. A
39. D
40. C
41. B
42. A
43. A

Test Practice Grade Five
Answer Key

P. 46–47
TEST 3: LANGUAGE MECHANICS/SPELLING (FORM A)
SAMPLE A: B
1. A
2. D
3. B
4. A
5. B
6. D
7. C
8. A
9. C
10. C
SAMPLE B: B
11. C
12. A
13. A
14. B
15. A
16. C
17. D
18. A
19. D
20. A

P. 48–51
TEST 3: LANGUAGE MECHANICS/USAGE (FORM A)
SAMPLE A: A
1. C
2. B
3. B
4. C
5. D
6. A
7. C
8. D
9. C
10. A
SAMPLE B: C
11. B
12. C
13. B
14. A
15. D
16. C
17. A
18. D
19. B
20. C
SAMPLE C: B
21. C
22. D
23. A
24. C
25. B
26. C
27. B
28. D

SAMPLE D: D
29. A
30. B
31. D
32. C
33. D

P. 52–53
TEST 4: LANGUAGE EXPRESSION (FORM A)
SAMPLE A: C
1. C
2. A
3. C
4. D
5. B
6. B
7. B
8. B
9. A
10. B
11. C
12. D

P. 54–55
TEST 3: LANGUAGE MECHANICS/SPELLING (FORM B)
SAMPLE A: D
1. A
2. C
3. B
4. C
5. A
6. C
7. D
8. B
9. C
10. B
SAMPLE B: A
11. B
12. B
13. C
14. D
15. A
16. B
17. D
18. B
19. A
20. C

P. 56–59
TEST 3: LANGUAGE MECHANICS/USAGE (FORM B)
SAMPLE A: C
1. A
2. C
3. B
4. D
5. B
6. A
7. C
8. D
9. B
10. A
SAMPLE B: D
11. D
12. A
13. B
14. B
15. C
16. B
17. C
18. B
19. A
20. C
SAMPLE C: B
21. B
22. A
23. C
24. B
25. C
26. C
27. C
28. D
SAMPLE D: B
29. A
30. C
31. D
32. A
33. C
34. B

P. 60–61
TEST 4: LANGUAGE EXPRESSION (FORM B)
SAMPLE A: C
1. D
2. A
3. C
4. D
5. A
6. C
7. B
8. D
9. A
10. B
11. C
12. D

P. 62–66
TEST 5: MATHEMATICS COMPUTATION (FORM A)
SAMPLE A: B
SAMPLE B: C
SAMPLE C: A
SAMPLE D: D
1. B
2. D
3. B
4. A
5. C
6. D
7. B
8. B
9. C
10. B
11. D
12. C
13. A
14. C
15. D
16. A
17. B
18. A
19. D
20. C
21. B
22. A
23. D
24. C
25. D
26. C
27. D
28. B
29. C
30. B
31. C
32. A
33. D
34. D
35. B
36. C
37. A
38. B
39. A
40. C

P. 67–71
TEST 5: MATHEMATICS COMPUTATION (FORM B)
SAMPLE A: C
SAMPLE B: B
SAMPLE C: D
SAMPLE D: A
1. A
2. C
3. A
4. B
5. C
6. A
7. C
8. A
9. C
10. B
11. B

Test Practice Grade Five
Answer Key

12. A
13. A
14. B
15. B
16. A
17. B
18. C
19. B
20. A
21. C
22. D
23. B
24. A
25. B
26. D
27. B
28. C
29. A
30. A
31. B
32. A
33. C
34. A
35. B
36. C
37. A
38. B
39. A
40. B

P. 72–73
TEST 6: MATHEMATICS CONCEPTS/APPLICATIONS: NUMERATION/NUMBER THEORY (FORM A)
SAMPLE A: C
SAMPLE B: A
1. C
2. B
3. A
4. A
5. C
6. A
7. C
8. D
9. A
10. C
11. A
12. B
13. B
14. A
15. B
16. D
17. B
18. C

P. 74–75
TEST 7: MATHEMATICS CONCEPTS/APPLICATIONS: GEOMETRY/MEASUREMENT (FORM A)
SAMPLE A: A
SAMPLE B: B
1. A
2. B
3. D
4. B
5. A
6. C
7. A
8. C
9. A
10. B
11. C
12. A

P. 76–77
TEST 8: MATHEMATICS CONCEPTS/APPLICATIONS: NUMBER SENTENCES/ RATIOS AND PERCENTS (FORM A)
SAMPLE A: C
SAMPLE B: A
1. A
2. B
3. A
4. C
5. A
6. C
7. D
8. B
9. C
10. B
11. A
12. B
13. D
14. A
15. C
16. B
17. B
18. B
19. D
20. B

P. 78–79
TEST 9: MATHEMATICS CONCEPTS/APPLICATIONS: READING CHARTS AND GRAPHS (FORM A)
SAMPLE: B
1. D
2. A
3. C
4. B
5. A
6. C
7. B
8. A
9. C
10. C

P. 80–81
TEST 6: MATHEMATICS CONCEPTS/APPLICATIONS: NUMERATION/NUMBER THEORY (FORM B)
SAMPLE A: A
SAMPLE B: C
1. B
2. C
3. B
4. B
5. C
6. C
7. C
8. B
9. D
10. A
11. C
12. A
13. C
14. A
15. A
16. C
17. B
18. A

P. 82–83
TEST 7: MATHEMATICS CONCEPTS/APPLICATIONS: GEOMETRY/MEASUREMENT (FORM B)
SAMPLE A: C
SAMPLE B: B
1. B
2. C
3. B
4. A
5. C
6. A
7. D
8. B
9. A
10. D
11. B
12. A

P. 84–85
TEST 8: MATHEMATICS CONCEPTS/APPLICATIONS: NUMBER SENTENCES/ RATIOS AND PERCENTS (FORM B)
SAMPLE A: B
SAMPLE B: C
1. A
2. A
3. B
4. A
5. C
6. B
7. D
8. B
9. A
10. B
11. B

P. 86–87
TEST 9: MATHEMATICS CONCEPTS/APPLICATIONS: READING CHARTS AND GRAPHS (FORM B)
SAMPLE: B
1. C
2. A
3. C
4. D
5. B
6. B
7. D
8. A
9. C
10. D

P. 88–94
TEST 10: MATHEMATICS PROBLEM-SOLVING (FORM A)
SAMPLE A: A
SAMPLE B: A
1. A
2. B
3. A
4. B
5. C
6. D
7. B
8. B
9. A
10. A
11. C
12. A
13. C
14. B
15. A
16. B
17. B
18. D
19. C
20. A
21. C
22. B

12. A
13. C
14. A
15. C
16. A
17. C
18. A
19. D
20. A

www.svschoolsupply.com
© Steck-Vaughn Company

127

Test Practice Grade Five
Answer Key

23.	C	29.	B	28.	D	24.	C
24.	B	30.	A	29.	B	25.	D
25.	D	31.	B	30.	A	26.	C
26.	A	32.	C	31.	C	27.	A
27.	C	33.	D	32.	B	28.	B
28.	B	34.	A	33.	A	29.	B
29.	D	35.	B	34.	C	30.	D
30.	A	36.	B	35.	B	31.	A
31.	B	37.	B	36.	A	32.	D
32.	C	38.	C	37.	C	33.	B
33.	B	39.	A	38.	A	34.	A
34.	B	40.	D	39.	C	35.	A
35.	A			40.	C	36.	D

P. 102–111
TEST 11: STUDY SKILLS (FORM A)

36.	A			41.	D	37.	B
37.	C			42.	A	38.	C
38.	B			43.	C	39.	C
39.	D			44.	B	40.	B
40.	A					41.	D

SAMPLE A: B
SAMPLE B: D
SAMPLE C: B
SAMPLE D: A

P. 95–101
TEST 10: MATHEMATICS PROBLEM-SOLVING (FORM B)

SAMPLE A: C
SAMPLE B: C

P. 112–122
TEST 11: STUDY SKILLS (FORM B)

SAMPLE A: C
SAMPLE B: D
SAMPLE C: A
SAMPLE D: C

TEST 10		TEST 11 A		TEST 11 B		cont.	
1.	A	1.	C	1.	C	42.	C
2.	C	2.	B	2.	A	43.	B
3.	B	3.	A	3.	D	44.	B
4.	C	4.	C	4.	A	45.	C
5.	A	5.	B	5.	B	46.	B
6.	C	6.	A	6.	C	47.	A
7.	A	7.	B	7.	B	48.	D
8.	B	8.	C	8.	A		
9.	C	9.	B	9.	D		
10.	B	10.	C	10.	C		
11.	A	11.	A	11.	A		
12.	D	12.	C	12.	C		
13.	C	13.	B	13.	B		
14.	D	14.	D	14.	C		
15.	B	15.	C	15.	A		
16.	D	16.	A	16.	D		
17.	C	17.	C	17.	A		
18.	A	18.	B	18.	A		
19.	C	19.	C	19.	C		
20.	A	20.	C	20.	C		
21.	A	21.	B	21.	D		
22.	C	22.	C	22.	C		
23.	C	23.	A	23.	B		
24.	B	24.	C				
25.	C	25.	A				
26.	C	26.	D				
27.	D	27.	A				
28.	D						